GE

MODEL CAR BUILDING

Dennis Doty

TAB BOOKS

Blue Ridge Summit, PA

Notices

Dremel is a registered trademark of Dremel Manufacturing, a division of Emerson Electric Co.
Floquil is a registered trademark and Polly S is a trademark of Floquil-Polly S Color Corp.
Hot Stuff and Super "T" are trademarks of Satellite City
Pactra is a registered trademark of Pactra Coatings, Inc., A Plasti-Kote Co.
Solvaset is a trademark of Hobsco, Inc.
3M is a registered trademark of Minnesota Mining and Manufacturing
X-Acto is a registered trademark of Hunt/X-Acto

FIRST EDITION
SECOND PRINTING

© 1989 by **TAB Books**.
TAB Books is a division of McGraw-Hill, Inc.

Library of Congress Cataloging-in-Publication Data

Doty, Dennis.
   Model car building.

   Bibliography: p.
   Includes index.
   1. Automobiles—Models. I. Title.
TL237.D683 1988   629.2′212   88-24794
ISBN 0-8306-9385-8 (pbk.)

TAB Books offers software for sale. For information and a catalog, please contact
TAB Software Department, Blue Ridge Summit, PA 17294-0850.

Contents

This book is respectfully dedicated to everyone who calls model cars his hobby or profession, with a special dedication to my parents, who have put up with so much for so long.

Introduction

I cannot remember the first model kit I ever built, but it seems like I have been building models forever. I do remember the first car kit I ever attempted to build. It was the Revell/AMT kit of the 1956 Ford Sunliner convertible, and it was in 1/32 scale. I was about 9 years old at the time, and I had not been building models for long. Construction did not go well because, unlike today, in 1956, most kits had multipiece bodies. My building experience had not yet reached the level needed to properly construct this kit.

Although the parts might have fit well, I could not get them to stay together, and I gave up on the model. Although I cannot remember for sure, I believe the problem was with me and not the kit. I think I tried to glue the plastic parts together with balsa cement. To say the least, that is not what you should use on a plastic kit.

Model car kits started to really come into their own in the late '50s. By 1960, I had stopped building airplanes and ships, and began concentrating on car models. To this day, no other type of model kit has really held my interest. It's been cars all the way.

Unfortunately, the model-car hobby sometimes suffers from a bad image. All too often when you let it be known that you are a collector and builder of model cars and you are over the age of 16, people tend to label you as someone who refuses to grow up. Thankfully, that opinion is changing as the hobby of building and collecting model cars continues to expand into the adult market.

Today, people from all professions are builders and collectors of model cars. Doctors, lawyers, politicians, and business executives enjoy the hobby. Your next-door neighbor might well be a model car builder and collector!

To my way of thinking, building model cars is the best of the construction hobbies. Few people travel on trains these days, and airplanes are still mainly for the mass transit of people. The automobile, however, is for the average person. The car touches almost everyone's life on a daily basis. The car is a form of transportation almost everyone can actually own. Not very many people can own a train or a plane.

For the car buff, the model car is about the only

way they can acquire a fleet of dream cars. Very few people are wealthy enough to own the classics with names like Duesenberg, Packard, and Bugatti; antiques like the Thomas Flyer, Mercer Raceabouts, and Stanley Steamers; or milestone cars like Studebakers, Corvettes, or Rivieras.

As a model car builder, all these famous marques are available to you. Through model cars, history can come to life before your eyes in a way that is better than all the pictures in a book—better even than visiting an automotive museum, because the model cars are yours. (That is basically why I am a model car builder and collector. What I could never afford in real vehicles, I have in model form.) And while it would likely be more fun to have the real vehicles, having the models is better than just having a picture of your favorite car.

Getting involved in building model cars is easier today than at any time in the past. For the most part, the kits being produced today are better and easier to build than earlier models. However, there are a growing number of kits on the market that the novice should not attempt to build. Even builders with moderate experience should let these kits go for a while. These kits have hundreds or even several thousand parts, and they are just beyond the scope of the novice. In fact, even the advanced builder will probably groan when he first opens the kit.

Looking at a kit like the one just mentioned is very humbling. It looks like it is impossible for all those parts to fit somewhere. All of them do have their place on the finished model, but don't think of the kit as a finished model. If you get to thinking of all the parts and how long the kit will take to assemble, you might never want to start.

Rather than thinking of the model as a whole, think of it only in terms of steps. Take each step one at a time. Before you know it, you will start to make real progress with the kit. Don't think of a model as a week, a month, or even a year away from completion. Think of getting the engine done, then the chassis, then the interior, and then the body. Then you can think of assembling the model and soon you will be done.

Another notion that is changing is that building and collecting model cars is strictly a hobby for males. Although there are few female participants, owning model cars is not a hobby that is restricted to males, any more than needlepoint is for "women only." Are you going to tell a big football player that needlepoint is only for women? Hobbies should have no stereotypes and should be enjoyed by everyone who has an interest in the subject.

Another point I would like to stress is that even if you read this book cover to cover 10 times, it will not make you a good model car builder. Building good model cars comes only with experience and by trial and error. Enjoy your success and learn from your errors. If you take the time to understand what you did wrong, you will learn more about building model cars from your errors than you will from your successes.

Painting your model cars is the one area that will probably take the most time to learn. It is the area modelers have the most trouble with, but it is also an area that can give you the most satisfaction once you have learned the art.

In 1961, I thought I was a pretty good builder. I had a couple of good friends who were also model car builders, and we were all at about the same skill level. Then one day, I decided to enter my models in the county fair. With the fair about a week away, I decided to make them a little better. I bought a can of spray paint to improve the looks of some of the models. I had no trouble learning to paint the models, and I thought they looked pretty good.

I arrived at the fair early and quickly set up my model cars. If I live to be 100 I will never forget what happened next. In walked this youngster about my age. As he unpacked his models and set them up, I am sure my jaw dropped to my feet. I had never seen anything so beautiful in my life. This was about the time Pactra had introduced its line of spray paints called 'namel paints. All of his cars were jewels, but the one that really caught my eye was AMT's 1936 Ford in candy apple red. That was the first time I ever *really* saw the model cars I had built: I wanted to crush them under my feet. It was only then that I realized I had painted 20 cars for the fair in blue Rust-Oleum! It looked like a fleet of *something*, and I wanted to die.

Needless to say, I didn't get the first-place

ribbon at that county fair. I have also known a few people who, after being similarly devastated, gave up on the hobby. They couldn't have cared much for it in the first place, because that episode gave me more drive than winning ever could have. I was determined to work at developing my skills and to achieve perfect paint jobs. I knew that it could be done. After all, I had seen them!

I worked very hard and spent a lot of money buying paint and kits to learn how to apply paint. It wasn't easy and it was expensive, but I did learn and I did improve my building skills. In fact, at the very next county fair I was able to take the first-place ribbon. It was a hollow victory, however, because the builder of that candy apple red 1936 Ford had moved out of town in the year between fairs.

When you come right down to it, that 1936 Ford is what turned me into a serious car modeler. Since then, I have always been working at making a better model with each car I build. And even though that incident with the 1936 Ford happened many years ago, I still remember it well and I still feel that I have

a lot more to learn about this hobby. Something new is always turning up to make the hobby more interesting. Those who think they know everything there is to know about building model cars really know very little. The better your skills become, the more skills there are to learn.

The main point I want to make is that you should not give up. If you enter a model contest and don't come out on top, take some time to look over the winning car and talk with the builder. In most contests, that car with the first-place ribbon or trophy deserved to win. Determine where you can improve your building skills and then work toward that goal. Try to build your next kit a little better and put a little more effort into it. Always try to make the next model a little better, even if only in a minor way, and you will eventually achieve the results you want. Before long, someone will be looking at your models and saying that they couldn't build model cars that looked like yours. But they can if they want to. After all, if it weren't for Willie Dixon and his candy apple red 1936 Ford, I probably wouldn't have written this book.

Chapter 1

A Brief History of Model Car Kits

Model car kits are not something new on the hobby scene. There were model car assembly kits in the 1930s and before. Most of these kits were little more than unassembled toys. Kits that resemble the ones we know were introduced right before the end of World War II (Fig. 1-1). In keeping with the times, these kits were military related and were made almost totally of wood. Plastic, the material that would change the hobby, was still several years down the road.

What follows is a very brief look at some of the kits and companies of the past. The kits mentioned have been off the hobby shop shelves for many years, and many of the companies that produced them are long gone, but because of the growing interest in older unbuilt kits, you would be surprised at how many of these older kits are starting to surface. Model car meets are springing up all over the country and are the best places for kit sellers to come in contact with kit buyers. Prices for many of the kits described in this chapter are beyond belief. On the other hand, some kits that are not in great demand are very reasonably priced.

Many factors determine the value of an old, unbuilt model car kit. Age is only one of these factors. If an old kit is not in great demand, age has little to do with value. The popularity of a kit is a much stronger determining factor. Although some of the balsa kits are very old, because their popularity is low, prices are also very reasonable for these kits. Some of the Revell Highway Pioneers are very common and are very inexpensive for kits so old.

Prices for original Highway Pioneers were further reduced when Minicraft Models, Inc., reissued many of the original Pioneers. These were reissued in four sets with four kits per set. The Cord and Duesenberg were reissued as separate kits, making these desirable (and high-priced) collectors' items available for the builder.

Generally, Corvettes, the "Pony" and muscle cars of the 60's, and the early annual kits are especially sought after, making them expensive if you want the originals. Original unbuilt kits are the most valuable, and always will be, but where once only an unbuilt kit had any real value to collectors, early annuals (1958 to 1962 especially) in built form now

1

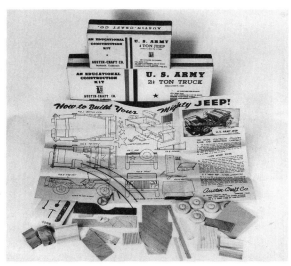

Fig. 1-1. World War II era kits included this 2 ½ truck kit and the ½-ton Jeep kit. Contents were mainly of wood.

memories for a few oldtime builders, if it weren't for some of these original kits still being in existence in their unbuilt form. It is unfortunate that so little is known of these early kit producers. When were the companies formed, when did they go out of business, what kits did they produce, and who founded them?

I know the histories of these companies would make interesting reading, but for the present time, the information is just not available. Only by reading sale lists and trading correspondence with other collectors do unusual items come to light. Anyway, at least a few examples of these kits exist and by examining them, a person can get at least a small idea of what the general hobby was like in its early days.

Two of the earliest producers of model car and truck kits were Austin-Craft (Fig. 1-1) and Megow. Austin-Craft's models were mainly hardwood construction with a few wire parts and a few detail items printed on a piece of paper. Even the wheels/tires in these kits were made of wood. The Austin-Craft and Megow kits came out before the close of World War II, and both models were of military vehicles. Megow's approach to the popular Jeep kit had a cardboard body and a few balsa wood parts with hardwood wheels/tires. Actually, using the body details printed on the cardboard, a built model of this kit should look fairly authentic.

The first model car manufacturer to really get the hobby going in the direction it has taken today was Hudson Miniatures. Its series of Old Timers in $\frac{1}{16}$ scale (Fig. 1-2) with balsa wood construction is what really sparked the interest of the early model car building public. Later kits had plastic parts, but the very early releases had wheels and small accessory parts in die-cast metal.

Hudson miniatures was started by A.J. Koveleski. His son, Oscar, is still one of the big names in the hobby. Oscar Koveleski helped found *Car Model Magazine* in 1962, and he founded Auto World in 1958. Auto World is still in the model car mail-order business today. A.J. Koveleski was a real car buff long before that hobby became as popular as it is today, and the Hudson Miniatures models

command prices that would have been high for an unbuilt example in 1980. Thankfully, resin reproductions of the original kits are again making these models available for those interested in building the cars. The resin kits are far from inexpensive, but they are much cheaper than the original kits (even in built form), and they are much easier to locate than an original kit in any form!

Many collectors believe it is better to leave old unbuilt kits in their unbuilt state, but kits were manufactured to be built, so don't hesitate to build an original collectors' kit. It is suggested, however, the collectors' kits not be attempted by a novice. There are a vast number of interesting car kits available today, and it is best for novice builders to hone their skills on these before tackling an original collectors' kit.

EARLY KITS

One of the earliest kits did not even have much wood in it. The basic material in the Megow kit was stiff precolored and die-cut cardboard.

Very little is known of these kits and of the companies that produced them. The companies are long out of business and most of the kits would be but

Fig. 1-2. One of the first post-World War II companies to get into hobby kits was Hudson Miniatures with its Old Timer kits: 1906 Columbia Electric (top), 1903 Rambler (middle left), 1900 Packard (middle right), 1902 Air Cooled Franklin (bottom left), 1903 Cadillac (bottom right).

were the kind of antique model cars A.J. Koveleski loved.

Success usually means imitation, and it wasn't long before its other companies started to produce model car kits. When a new company releases its first kits, the designers usually try to make an improvement on the earlier kits so that the public will buy their kits over the kits of the older manufacturer. Similar in construction to the Hudson Miniatures, the kits from the Fador company were known as Smallsters. There were some minor changes over earlier balsa-based kits, but not that much improvement. A rare truck model from Ting, an obscure British firm, was also offered at the same time.

Not all companies produced models of antique cars. Companies like Ace (Fig. 1-3) started making

1/24-scale models of more current autos. Like the other model car companies of the time, Ace did stick with basic balsa construction material, but the tires were made of a rubberlike compound. Ace models included many current car kits and a popular series of (then) state-of the-art hot rods.

Although the way it was done could hardly be called an improvement, the F-B kits (Fig. 1-4) did contain a sheet of stamped aluminum parts. These parts simulated the chrome pieces, but the modeler had to cut them from the sheet. These F-B models were the crudest balsa model car kits produced. Producing a realistic model from one of the kits from this company was some accomplishment.

At the opposite end of the scale from the F-B models was Berkeley Models. Balsa was still the

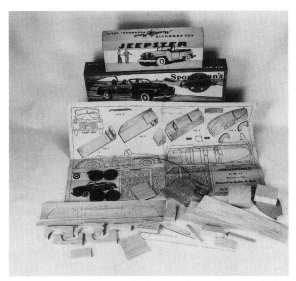

Fig. 1-3. It wasn't long before modern cars were being made into kit form. The Ace company was one of the first with kits like these ¼4-scale Jeepster and Ford Sportsman convertible.

main material and the rubber tires were no improvement over those from Ace. Berkeley did give the model car builder die-cast metal parts for the grilles, bumpers, and some accessory parts (Fig. 1-5). These models were made to ¼4 scale, and they were available throughout the 1950s.

Plastics opened up the model car hobby to the mass public. Plastic parts could be found in the Hudson Miniatures and Smallster kits, but only as accessory parts. Balsa and hardwoods took a while to die out, even though kits kept getting more plastic parts. Examples are the 1877 Selden Patient Wagon from Mod-Ac Models and the very rare Railway Express truck from Continental (Fig. 1-6). The first all-plastic model cars were released under the Revell banner, and were called Highway Pioneers.

This series of ⅓2-scale cars (Fig. 1-7) is what really started the model car craze that is still going strong today. It is not too hard to see why plastic kits were so popular from the start. With a wood model, a great deal of time was required to come

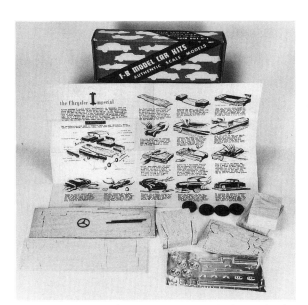

Fig. 1-4. Most challenging modern car kits had to be the crude F-B's kits. Balsa was the main material, but also included was a sheet of stamped aluminum for bumpers and trim parts. Shown is Chrysler Imperial.

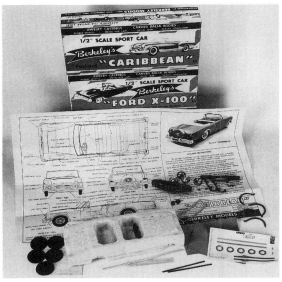

Fig. 1-5. Berkeley's balsa-based kits were probably best of the wood car kits. Basic body was a block of wood, rough-cut to shape; kit included cast metal parts (very well done) for bumpers. Shown are the Packard Caribbean (top) and the experimental Ford X-100 (bottom).

up with a completed model. Balsa kits took a lot of time to finish because it is a very porous material and needs a lot of priming and sanding to produce a finished product. With plastic, about all a person had to do was carefully assemble the parts. Usually this process took just a few hours. Most of these kits came molded in colors. These early kits were not molded in the same way that plastic kits are molded today. Most of the early plastic kits were molded in acetate, and acetone was needed to bond the parts together.

Revell released about 31 models in the 1/32-scale Highway Pioneers series. The series covered cars from the earliest days of motoring to the then modern cars of the early '50s. Also included were a few hot rods.

The Highway Pioneers were issued three different times. The boxes for the first release kits had drawings of the five different cars in the series, and there were four series for the first release. The original Highway Pioneer kits were molded in acetate. Revell also released these series in sets with all the cars of a series in one box. The box resembled the smaller boxes, but naturally it was bigger to hold the five kits in the series. The sets are es-

pecially hard to find today, but the original single releases are not at all hard to obtain.

I have never seen any cars beyond these first four series in the original-style box, but that is not to say the later releases were never in the original-style boxes.

The style of the second release of the original Highway Pioneers had a change in plastic from acetate to styrene. Although both types of plastic could be found in these boxes, it's likely the earliest releases had the molded acetate parts, and the kits with styrene were likely issued a little later.

Because the boxes are different than the original release, these kits are easy to distinguish. The new boxes had a drawing of just the one car in the box. The new box art wasn't the only difference; these releases had improved parts in them. Some of the more impressive releases, such as the

Fig. 1-7. The company that got the ball rolling with plastic kits was Revell, with the release of Gowland and Gowland-produced models, called Highway Pioneers. Shown are four series of kits with five different models in each series. These are the original releases in the series; displayed is 1915 Ford 'T' Sedan.

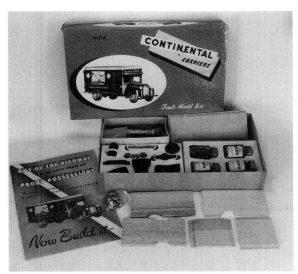

Fig. 1-6. Continental Products also released wood and plastic kits. This very rare model of a Railway Express truck had many well-detailed plastic parts.

Duesenberg and 810 Cord, were issued for the first time. Note that no Highway Pioneer kit ever came with plated parts.

The last release for these kits, the third issue, came in the late '50s, early '60s. Gone was all reference to Gowland & Gowland, and the complete series of cars was not reissued. Only selected models, most likely the proven best-sellers, were available. The boxes were bigger and the art was more colorful. Like the second release, only the car in the box was shown on the cover. All the kits in the third release were molded in styrene. Kits from this series are shown in Fig. 1-8.

Soon, Hudson Miniatures had a series of cars to compete with the Revell Highway Pioneers. Unlike their $\frac{1}{16}$-scale balsa kits, the new kits from Hudson Miniatures were plastic, and also in $\frac{1}{32}$ scale, just like the Revell cars. However, the Lil' Old Timers, as Hudson Miniatures called their cars, were better detailed than the original Highway Pi-

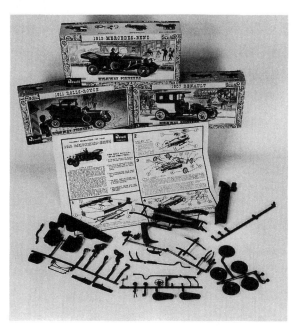

Fig. 1-8. In the late '50s, Revell once again reissued some of the Highway Pioneers. These boxes were larger and all the kits were molded in styrene plastic. Shown on top is the 1913 Mercedes-Benz, with the 1911 Rolls Royce on the left, 1907 Renault on the right.

oneers. (Revell subsequently made some die and parts improvements, most likely because of the Lil' Old Timers.) Unfortunately, Hudson Miniatures released only five of the eight announced kits. It is also interesting to note that Revell bought the tooling for these five Lil' Old Timers, releasing them in Great Britain only.

The next important step in the evolution of the model car kit was the Revell/AMT kits of 1955 and 1956 cars in $\frac{1}{32}$ scale (Fig. 1-9). After many questions and a lot of digging for answers, the relationship between these two companies remains a mystery. While it is not yet known for sure why these two companies joined forces for this very interesting series of kits, I would like to make a guess. AMT had been producing model cars for the auto industry. Revell, on the other hand, had been producing kits for several years. Revell had the kit experience, and AMT had the contacts with the real car companies. I assume they joined forces to bring their respective experience to the creation of a modern model car kit. The kits were a complete success.

The kits were all styrene plastic and contained some of the first chrome-plated parts used in the hobby. The parts were highly detailed and the models had very well-detailed engines. In many ways, the detail on these kits is better than some kits being produced today. The only drawback these kits had was their multi-piece bodies. This made the construction a bit harder for the novice builder. As for detail, these kits lacked nothing.

The next milestone was in 1957, when Revell released some car kits in $\frac{1}{25}$ scale. AMT had been using the $\frac{1}{25}$ scale for their models from the start, but this was the first time Revell had car kits in this scale. Their release of the 1957 Cadillac Eldorado Brougham and 1957 Ford Country Station Wagon were immediate successes (Fig. 1-10). Only the Brougham was lacking in every detail, because it did not contain a scale engine. Both kits still had the multi-piece bodies. Both kits are highly sought after collectors' items and very hard to find. Revell converted the Ford from a wagon to the Ranchero in about 1960 (non-stock).

The first model car from AMT was a 1948 Ford, cast in aluminum, reflecting the company's name:

Fig. 1-9. (above) The real breakthrough in modern kits in plastic came with the Revell/AMT 1955 and 1956 kits in ⅟₃₂ scale: 1956 Continental Mark II (top left), and 1956 Mercury (top right), 1956 Cadillac (middle left), 1956 Chrysler (middle), 1956 Buick (middle right), 1955 Cadillac (bottom left), 1955 Chrysler (bottom middle), and 1955 Buick (bottom right). Note the 1956 Buick is a later edition without the AMT logo.

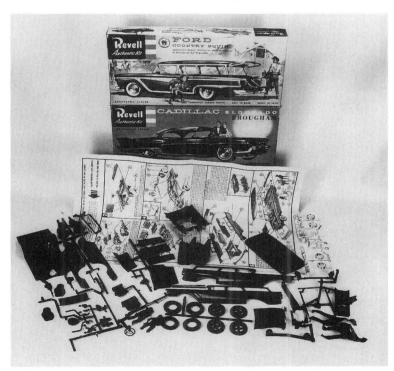

Fig. 1-10. (right) In 1957, Revell released two of the most sought after ⅟₂₅-scale collectors' items, the 1957 Ford Country Squire Station Wagon and 1957 Cadillac Eldorado Brougham.

Aluminum Model Toys. In 1949, they switched to a Kodak plastic called *Tenite* (an acetate), and the plastic model car era was born.

The early AMT plastic models were not kits. They were used by the auto industry as promotional models that had been produced in the correct colors of the real cars. AMT also released these promo models to the toy trade as wind-up models and remote control toys.

Exactly when AMT released its first kit is a matter of debate. It depends on what a person considers a kit. In 1953, the company released a "kit" of the 1953 Ford convertible with Indy race car decals. Also in 1953, AMT released the first of a set of three cars in a box that contained paint. This was known as a *two-tone kit*. All these "kits" were unassembled promotional model cars. These kits are probably the first true AMT kits. Their heritage, however, really goes back to the unassembled toys of the '30s, rather than to the hobby kits of the time.

For most hobbyists, AMT's 3-in-1 kits of 1958 are considered AMT's first true kits. These kits were still little more than an unassembled promo-

tional item, but this time the kits were molded in styrene plastic and had a one-piece body. The kits did not come with a hood that opened and engine detail, but AMT did include extra custom parts, extra racing parts, and some decals. The 1959 kits were just about the same, but in 1960, some of the AMT annual kits had detailed engines. Engines were offered in the Buick, Thunderbird, and Corvette kits; while the Chevy Apache and Ford F-100 Pickups were new to the kit line, they also contained engines and even a trailer—they were really something for 1960! AMT released the kits in ¹⁄₂₅ scale (Fig. 1-11).

Almost as important in the history of the model car as the AMT yearly 3-in-1 kits were the introduction of the first in a long line of kits to be called the Trophy series. The first release was in 1959, and it was the very popular 1932 Ford Model B Roadster. This model could be built as a stock 1932 Ford Roadster or as a really sharp street rod with a Chrysler Hemi engine.

For those too young to remember, 3-in-1 stood for the versions that could be built from the one kit; stock, custom (or rod), and racing. The second re-

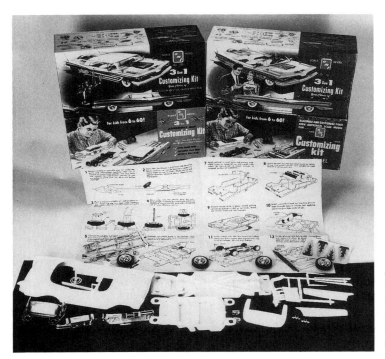

Fig. 1-11. The 1958 AMT ¹⁄₂₅-scale kits evolved into the modern plastic kit we know today. In the photograph are the 1958 (lower boxes) and 1959 style kits. Hardtops and convertibles came in different box styles.

lease in the series was a 1932 Ford V-8 five-window (Deuce) Coupe.

These releases were quickly followed by such kits as the 1940 Ford coupe, the 1939/1940 Ford Sedan, the 1932 Ford Sports Roadster and the 1936 Ford Roadster/chopped-top Coupe (Fig. 1-12). Around 1960, AMT released the first double kit in the Trophy series. The 1925 Ford T could be built as a roadster or a chopped-top coupe. One could be built stock, and the other one could be built custom.

Another double kit soon followed. The Double Dragster kit had enough parts to build two complete dragsters. The greatest kit AMT has ever released, in terms of popularity, is the 1957 Chevy. Many of the kits in the Trophy series are still being made by AMT, but not in the original form. All of the kits have been updated to a certain extent.

Another company that produced promotional model cars for the auto industry (and frictions and remote control toys for the toy trade) was Jo-Han Models. Jo-Han was founded in the '40s by John Haenle, Jr. The company produced many toy and promotional items under the Ideal Model banner until 1955. The first Jo-Han kits were for 1959 models, and they were pretty much like the kits AMT released in 1958. Basically, they were unassembled promos with decals and a few custom parts. The big change in Jo-Han models came in 1962, when some of them included detailed engines and when the first convertibles were released (Fig. 1-13).

In the late '50s and early '60s, Hubley was the only company producing diecast metal kits. The series contained Ford Model As, 1932 Chevys, Duesenbergs, and Packards. The tooling came under the Gabriel banner in the '70s and several Model T Fords were added to the line. Many of these metal kits are now being produced by Scale Models. Two metal kits not reissued by Hubley, Gabriel, or Scale

Fig. 1-12. Early AMT Trophy series kits: Left column, top: first Trophy kit, 1932 Ford Roadster. Under this is the 1932 Ford Coupe, and under that is the 1932 Ford Sports Roadster. Right column, top: 1940 Ford Coupe, under this is the 1940 Ford Sedan, and under that, the 1936 Ford Roadster with a chopped coupe top.

Models (to date, at least) are the Indy Racer and the (so-called) 1932 Ford roadster (Fig. 1-14); both kits are based on the same chassis, with the 1932 Ford having a more late "T" look to it.

Although Hubley is well known for its metal kits, it is not so well known for the excellent plastic kits the company produced during the late '50s and early '60s. The best models in this series were the sporting cars. The open cars came in two versions. One had an open top and one had the top in place. These kits are rather hard to find today. Entex did reissue the Rolls Royce, Triumph TR-3, and Mercedes 300SL Roadster, but none of the other kits made it. Revell of Europe also had these kits in their line for a number of years.

Hubley also made promotional models for the Ford Motor company. Like most other promotional producing companies, Hubley also released these promos as unassembled kits. These kits were not all that popular then because the Fords being modeled were the low-priced Fairlane 500 four-door sedan and Country Sedan Station Wagon, and during the early '60s, four-door models and station wagon kits were not all that popular. The 1962 Ford wagon is the rarest model of the bunch. All the Hubley plastic kits were produced in 1/24 scale.

Monogram Models Inc., founded by Jack M. Besser and Robert Reder, is another company with a long history in the model field (Fig. 1-15). Monogram's first kits were molded in acetate. Because of this, they do tend to warp in time. Most of the early Monogram car kits were of hot rods and dragsters with an Indy car for good measure. Of the early Monogram kits, the most desirable to the collectors are the 1955 and 1956 Cadillacs. These kits were made in both hardtop and convertible form for 1955, with only the convertible available for 1956. These Monogram Cadillacs were produced to 1/20 scale.

Fig. 1-13. Jo-Han got into kits in 1959. In 1960 and 1961, kit boxes were all the same, though 1961 kits had photos of the car on the box. 1962 kits were similar but this was the first year for a Jo-Han convertible, so there were boxes for hardtops and convertibles.

Because the ½20-scale 1955 Cadillacs were molded in acetate plastic, they tend to warp more so than the models in ½25 scale. Not all of them have warped, and some examples are truly beautiful models. They are state of the art for the time they were produced. Along with the Revell/AMT 1955 kits, the Monogram 1955 Cadillacs were among the first kits to have parts plated in a chromelike finish. I have seen an example of the 1956 Cadillac that has plating to rival any being produced today.

In the early '60s, Monogram produced a series of very well detailed and highly desirable kits. Their 1955 Chevy, which could be built as either a hardtop or convertible, is regarded as a classic kit of the era. Because this kit was altered in the early '70s to make it a street racer, it is doubtful if it will ever be back in its original form. A special feature of all Monogram kits is the very glossy plastic. This is achieved by highly polishing the molds, and it is a Monogram trademark.

Large-scale kits started to become very popular during the 1970s, but they have been around since the '50s. One of the first companies to make large-scale plastic kits was the Ideal Toy Corporation (ITC). This company produced a 1953-55 Corvette, an Olds convertible (about 1954 vintage), and a Thunderbird (about 1955 vintage). No scale was listed of these kits, but they were in the ½12 to ½10 size.

In the early '60s, Renwall released a ¼-scale kit of an engine called The Visible V-8, and they also made a visible chassis to go with it. Monogram released a Chevy customizing engine kit in ½8-scale, and Revell released a highly detailed model of the new Chrysler Slant Six engine in ¼ scale.

Later, Monogram put their engine kit into a complete model called the Big T. This was a ½8-scale model of a '20s Ford T street rod. Lindberg Models (founded in 1933 by Paul A. Lindberg) released a ½8-scale rail dragster with double engines and followed this up with kits in ½12 and ½16 scale. ITC also released a few interesting larger scale kits in the '60s. One was a Mercer Raceabout in what must be close to ½8-scale (Fig. 1-16), and a Duesenberg Roadster in about the same.

Fig. 1-14. Late '50s also saw the start of metal-bodied kits, with Hubley being one of the first. This 1932 Ford Roadster more resembled a 1927 Model T Ford and was based on their earlier release of the Indy 500 Roadster. All plastic parts were molded in clear.

Fig. 1-15. Monogram released a great many plastic kits in the '50s. The '60s saw the release of items like the 1930 Ford Model Phaeton (left), 1930 Ford Coupe/Cabrolet (top right), and 1936 Ford Coupe/Cabrolet (bottom right).

Fig. 1-16. In the early '60s, several companies started releasing kits in much larger scales. This Mercer Raceabout by ITC listed no scale, but was almost ⅛. There was no engine, but it could be operated with the use of an electric motor.

MPC

Model Products Corporation (MPC) was founded by George Toteff, one of the early driving forces behind AMT. The first MPC kit was a 1964 Corvette Coupe (Fig. 1-17). MPC is the latest of the major car model building companies to be founded, but some of their kits are already highly prized collectors' items.

A LOOK AT SCALES

Throughout this chapter, I have mentioned scales. Actually, the terms I used—1/32, 1/25, 1/24—are really not the scales of model cars. They are the proportions. A 1/32-scale car is really 1/32 the size of a real car. You could think of a real car being 32 times as large as the model. To be exact, the scale of a 1/32-size model is 3/8 inch to 1 foot, or just 3/8 inch scale. That might have been used years ago, and it is still technically correct, but it is just never used today by any of the manufacturers or the builders. Every-

Fig. 1-17. MPC was one of the last major companies to start producing model cars. Their first kit was the 1964 Corvette Coupe (lower left). They updated the Corvette to a 1965 and added a few new makes to the line like the 1965 Dodge Monaco hardtop and 1965 Dodge 880 convertible. The line was expanded still more in 1966, with that year being represented by the rare GTO convertible.

one uses just plain old 1/32, 1/25, 1/24, and all the other *scales*.

To get a better idea of what scale is all about and how it relates to a model car, examine Fig. 1-18. The models used in this photo are all of the same basic car: a 1974 to 1979 Corvette Coupe. The difference in the length of the models is the difference in scales. The difference in length of the 1/8-scale Monogram Corvette and the Corvette in near HO scale from Mid America's Collectors Case Inc. is amazing. The lines on the photo are drawn to the exact length of the cars even though it doesn't always look like it because of the angle the photo was taken.

HOW MODEL CARS ARE MADE

I think it is important for you to understand what goes into producing a model car kit so you will have a bit better idea of why certain kits are made and why others are not.

The model car kit you see on the hobby shop shelves starts with a simple idea. Someone thinks a certain car, in kit form, would be a good selling model. This idea can come from a planner within a model company, or it can come from someone writing a letter saying that they would like a specific car modeled.

From this proposal stage, the model being considered is studied to see if the model would be a good commercial kit to release. Translation: will it make money? If the powers that be within the company feel that it would be a good selling kit, the idea moves to the next stage.

If the proposed model is of a real car (as it almost always is today), the model company will locate a real car and take hundreds of photos and measurements of everything on the car. No part is left out. Sometimes the model company can obtain the actual drawings used by the automobile manufacturer, and the scale drawings are made from the plans for the real car.

Once scale drawings are made of all the parts that will be in the kit, they are given to skilled workers in the wood shop. Here the pieces of the kit are made in wood to 1/10 scale. These wood patterns are just like the finished kit. The better these are made, the better the model kit will be.

These wood patterns are then taken to the tool makers, where the parts are reduced to the correct scale and cut into steel molds by a pantograph machine. When the steel molds are finished, they are placed in large injection molding machines (costing several hundred thousand dollars) and several test shots are run to see how the molds work.

These test shots are checked to make sure the molds all fill with plastic, to make sure the molds all line up, and to check for other potential problems. Some of these test shots are built up to make sure all parts fit correctly. If the parts do not fit together correctly, the molds are modified and more test shots are run. Once again, the parts are checked for fit. When all is well with these molds, they are removed from the molding machine and are given their final detailing (if necessary) and then they are

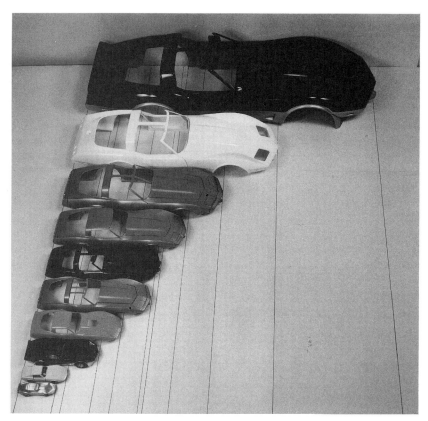

Fig. 1-18. The back model is the 1/8-scale Monogram 1978 Corvette. The next model is the 1978 Corvette by Otaki in 1/12 scale. Next is the 1978 Corvette in 1/16 scale by MPC. The fourth model from the back is the 1/20-scale 1979 Corvette by MPC. Next is the 1/24-scale Monogram 1978 Corvette followed by the 1/25-scale 1978 Corvette by MPC. The next model in line is the 1/32-scale 1978 Corvette snap kit by Monogram. That is followed by the 1978 Corvette Pace car by Nostalgic Miniatures/Miniature Toys Inc. in 1/43 scale. It is followed by the 1/64-scale 1977 Corvette by Tomica. The last Corvette shown is the near HO scale (1/87 is true H.O.) 1978 Corvette Pace Car from Mid America Enterprises (and cast in pewter). All these models are of a car that is the same length. The only change is the scale in which they are manufactured.

highly polished. The molds are again installed in the molding machines, and the kits are run.

While all the tooling is taking place, other people are working on other areas of the kit. Instruction sheets must be made up and box art prepared. Then both items must be printed.

The actual production of a model car kit starts out with raw plastic. After plastic has been heated to a liquid stage, it is fed into an injection molding machine. The injection of the liquid plastic into the molds is made under very high pressure. Otherwise, the plastic would quickly cool, and the mold would not fill up. Once the plastic has been injected, water is used to cool the mold and solidify the plastic so that the parts can be removed from the mold.

At this stage, the molding machine operator usually bags the still warm parts while keeping separate the parts that are to be chromed. The bagged parts are placed in large boxes to be assembled into complete kits later.

The parts to be plated are attached to racks and then either sprayed or dipped in a special, nearly clear liquid so that they can be vacuum plated. Before they can be plated, however, they must be heat dried in a special oven. From the drying oven, the racks are transferred to even larger racks.

Small strips of aluminum are placed on electrical wires on this rack, and the rack is placed in the vacuum machine. Air and moisture are pumped from the machine. When this stage is achieved, the racks are spun, and a strong electrical current is passed through the wires over which the aluminum strips were draped. This melts the aluminum. In the vacuum, the vaporized aluminum is attracted to the specially sprayed plastic parts, and the parts are "chrome" plated. The vacuum is released in the plating machine, and the plated parts are removed from the machine. Next, the racks are unloaded, and the plated parts are sent to the assembly area.

From this stage, all the kit components are brought together in the kit box. Sometimes this is done automatically, and sometimes the separate components are assembled by hand. Once all the parts are in the kit box, the carton lid is put in place and the completed kit is heat shrunk in its plastic wrapper. The individual kits are then boxed. What started as only an idea a year or so ago is now a completed model car ready to be sent to the hobby shop and then home to your collection.

The process from an idea to a kit on the hobby shop shelf is a long and costly one. A mold that cost $20,000 or so to tool up in the early '60s would now cost at least $150,000. And even at that, $150,000 is not considered an expensive tool by today's standards. So if you are wondering why the price of a model kit went from $1.49 in 1960 to the current price of over $7.00, that is one of the reasons. Plastic is a petroleum-based chemical, and the costs of the basic material of the kit has increased tremendously as the price of oil has risen. It really isn't so much a matter of a kit being so expensive, but rather a matter of how the companies can produce as inexpensively as they do.

Chapter 2

Tools

Tools are a necessity for building any model car. Even a snap together kit cannot be built correctly—without the probability of damaged parts—unless you have at least one tool; the X-Acto knife.

KNIVES AND BLADES

The most useful tool for building models that you will ever buy is the #1 X-Acto knife handle with a #11 blade. One knife will be enough for beginners, but this is an inexpensive item, and I strongly suggest that you eventually get at least three of the #1 handles. For the work I do, I have one knife with a new blade in it at all times. I use this knife only for cutting Bare-Metal Foil.

The second knife is my general purpose work knife. The third knife is used for the dirty jobs, and the jobs that would dull my second knife too much. The third knife is used to spread body putty, cut aluminum tubing, and similar jobs. As the blade in the first knife gets dull with use, I replace that blade with a new one. Because the blade from the first knife is still very sharp, I transfer the blade to the second knife for my general hobby use. The blade I take out of the second knife is by this time usually pretty dull, but it is more than good enough for the messy work I do with the third knife, and that is where the blade from my second knife goes. The old blade in the third knife, by now very dull and usually caked with dried body putty, is still not discarded. I place it where I can get at it if I need it for any reason.

All this makes a single blade go a very long way, and at the same time, you always have the best blade for the job whenever it is needed. Better yet, you don't dull a new blade with general hobby work. Keeping the knives separated so that you know which is which is no problem either. If you have a permanent workbench, make up some kind of holders for the knives and always return them to their same location. When you have several knives on the workbench at the same time, it could cause a slight problem. Which is your number one knife and where is number three? This problem can be solved by using a tubing cutter to make identifying marks on the knives.

The first knife handle I leave as it comes from the factory. Using the tube cutter to cut the groove, I score the second handle with one ring near the end of the handle. Don't cut a deep groove, just go around the handle a couple of times with the tube cutter. The tube cutter will usually leave a slight ridge that should be filed or sanded smooth.

On the third handle, I cut two grooves close to each other. This way I know what knife has what blade in it at all times. Actually, I do have more than three #1 X-Acto handles. I also have a fourth handle with a #13 saw blade in it. This fourth handle can also save you a lot of time and should be considered.

The #11 X-Acto blade will serve your model car needs about 90 percent of the time. The #13 saw blade will work in most of the other cases. At rare times, you might need a specially shaped blade, and it is nice to know that X-Acto makes blades in many styles for many different handles (Fig. 2-1). Because these blades are not going to be used all that much, your best bet would be to pick up assortment pack #11 and a package of #16 blades. The styles in these packages will be the ones you are most likely to use. X-Acto makes several styles of handles for their blades. Examine them at a hobby shop or send for a catalog so that you know what is available in case a special job that needs a special handle comes up.

PAINTBRUSHES

If there is anything on which you shouldn't try to save money, it is paintbrushes. Inexpensive brushes might be adequate if they are not used very often, but they just do not hold up under general hobby use. In looking over the brushes I have, the name M. Grumbacher seems to appear most frequently. They produce a wide variety of brushes that hold

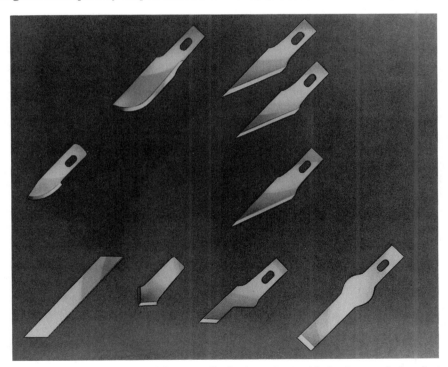

Fig. 2-1. If you are building your first model, you really don't need extra blades for your knives just yet. Extra #11 blades (upper right) are good to have. As you advance, another blade you will need is the #13 saw (lower left), used for many operations.

up very well in all hobby applications. For general painting, the round tipped brush will serve you well. Get this in several sizes from about the #4 to #8 size or larger if the need arises. Flat brushes are good for painting wide areas that can be brush painted. It is best to have several sizes on hand. Fine pointed brushes are required for small detailing. They range in size from the smallest, 00000, to about a 00 for slightly larger areas.

Maintaining the point on detail brushes is very important. After you have cleaned the paint out of the brush, wet your finger and twirl the brush on the finger you wet to work the brush back to a perfect point. Let the brush dry before using it again.

Brushes are expensive, and if you buy all you could need at one time, you will be spending a bundle. You usually don't need all the sizes at one time, so just get a couple each week (or as the need arises). Before you know it, you will have all the brushes you need.

Cleaning the Brushes

Brushes will last a lot longer if they are kept clean. Get a small empty jar and a quart (or so) of paint thinner. Fill the small jar with thinner and clean the brush by dipping it in the thinner and rolling the bristles against the side of the glass jar. This gets the thinner through the brush and does a very good job of cleaning it. When the brush is cleaned, wipe the thinner out of it with a paper towel.

For the best results, however, use a two-step method for cleaning your brushes. The first jar of thinner is used to clean the brushes right after painting, when the brushes have the most paint in them. You can prolong the use of this first thinner by removing excess paint from the brush by wiping it with a paper towel before putting it into the thinner. Now clean the brush as first described. Instead of putting the brush away after cleaning it in the first jar of thinner, clean the brush in a second jar of thinner. This second cleaning will remove additional paint. When the thinners are too filled up with paint, discard them and put fresh thinner in the jars.

The two-bath system works well for cleaning brushes used to apply enamel paints, but it will not work well for lacquer paints you sometimes need to brush on (usually for touch-up). Here lacquer thinner could be used, but I prefer to use acetone to clean the brushes after painting with lacquers. Acetone is a powerful solvent and should be used only with great care. It must also be used in a well-ventilated area because of the strong fumes. Acetone and lacquer thinners are not the best for brushes, and they will shorten their life, but I haven't had that much trouble with the Grumbacher line of brushes when I clean them with acetone.

Other Uses For Paintbrushes

In time, even the best paintbrush will wear out. The bristles will fall out, the tip will deteriorate, or the brush might even break because of abuse. Do not throw the brush away, however, because it still has a useful life—but not as a paintbrush. Cut off any bristles that remain, and the handle can be used as a holder when painting a number of items.

Storage Of Paintbrushes

To ensure the maximum life of a paintbrush, never store it with the bristles down so that the weight of the brush is on the bristles. This will distort their shape and render the brush useless. Store the brush so that the bristles are pointing up or store the brush on its side.

RAZOR SAW BLADES

For long straight cuts, X-Acto razor saw blades are what you need. X-Acto also makes a handle for these blades. I don't prefer to use the saws with the handle, but I find that it is a very useful handle for other applications. Many types of blades will work in it.

The blades come separately, but I would suggest getting the razor saw set with the handle and a #234 and a #255 saw blade. That way you will not only have the most useful razor saw blades, but also the handle when it is needed.

FILES

I strongly suggest that you get a set of needle files so that you will have all the types of small files you will need. Having the right file for the job is very important. You should also have a set of X-Acto miniature files for model car work. These very small files will get much use. When used on plastic only, these hobby files will last a very long time.

I also suggest that you shop the hardware store for a larger mill bastard file. These long flat files are ideal for filing long flat surfaces. The file I work with most is 8 inches long and not too coarse. A file handle is a nice accessory for this type of file. Several sizes of larger round files are also items you should pick up while you are at the hardware store.

RULERS

Metal rulers that are 6 or 12 inches long are also very useful items. General makes a 6-inch ruler with a pocket clip that is especially recommended. The General ruler can be found in some hobby shops, but hardware stores are a better source.

SANDPAPER

Sandpaper in all grades and types is another tool you can hardly be without. For general sanding, use a rather fine grit (as compared to that used to sand a real car), no-load sandpaper. My preference in this is made by Armour and it is called Armoshield—a silicon carbide paper. it comes in several grades that don't seem as coarse as other types of sandpaper. The grades I use most often are 150 and 250. Unfortunately, Armour sandpaper is not the easiest to find. Try the automotive paint stores along with any of the better hardware stores in your area. Because it is harder to find, I suggest stocking up on it when you do find it.

Another must item for model car hobbyists is 400-grit and 600-grit wet or dry sandpaper. This paper is usually available in hardware stores and some hobby shops as well as automotive paint stores. For finishing model work, use it wet. Have a container of water to dip the paper in and wipe the body you are sanding every now and then. After doing a lot of body work, it is usually a good idea to sand with 400-grit paper (wet) before priming to smooth the rough sanding. Then use 600-grit paper to sand the prime down. At times, you will also need the advantage of a really fine sandpaper. For this, I take

regular 600-grit paper and sand it against itself (lightly) to make a really fine wet sandpaper.

Since the first edition of this book was written, much finer grades of sandpaper have been produced. Grit numbers as fine as 12,000, which is finer than you would need for any normal sanding, are now available. Grits this fine are desirable for the final polishing of your paint jobs.

TWEEZERS

You should have at least a few tweezers. Find the ones with the most pointed tips. Tweezers with a bit more of a blunt end are also useful. Another type of tweezer that has limited applications, but are hard to do without when the need for them arises, are self-closing tweezers. These tweezers are very useful when you want to clamp parts together.

PLIERS

Another tool that is hard to do without is pliers. You should have at least two and at least one of those should be a long-nose (also known as needle-nose) pliers. Regular household pliers also come in handy, as do diagonal cutting pliers. Two pairs of the long-nose pliers are nice to have, and the second set does not have to be purchased right away.

X-Acto makes many kinds of useful pliers. Know what is available so that you can get them as they are needed. In many ways, it is best to wait almost until you need a tool to buy it. Otherwise you will be spending so much on tools that you won't be able to afford to buy a model car kit.

TUBE CUTTER

If you plan to be working with brass tubing, a tube cutter that will cut tubing as small as $1/16$-inch in diameter is a necessity. Most hobby shops that carry tubing will also carry a tubing cutter. Aluminum tubing can be cut without a tube cutter; by simply rolling the tube on a smooth flat surface with the edge of a #11 X-Acto blade, you can usually cut aluminum tubing to length. Roll the tubing carefully or you won't get a straight cut. Work slowly or when you cut through the tube, it might go flying. Aluminum tubing is soft, and it can be cut with a regular #11 blade, but it will quickly dull the blade. Use a blade that is dull to begin with when you are cutting aluminum tubing.

PUNCHES

Punches are very handy items for making holes in softer items like paper, cardboard, or plastic that is up to about .040 of an inch thick. X-Acto makes punches for several of their handles, but only in the 3/16- and 1/2-inch sizes. Refer to Chapter 6 for information on how to make punches in other sizes.

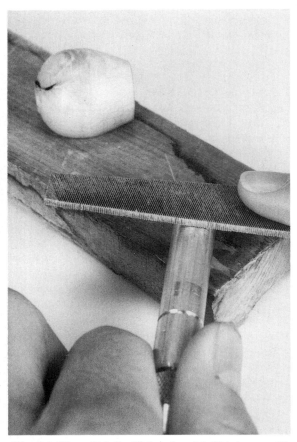

Fig. 2-2. To modify the X-Acto hand drill into one with a swivel head, first carefully remove the wooden head. File the knurled end flush with the shaft of the drill.

SCREWDRIVERS

Many of the more advanced kits and most of the metal kits come with screws. Older kits also had the body secured to the chassis with screws. Screwdrivers are not expensive, and you would do well to have a set of small screwdrivers on hand. Screwdrivers in a larger size should also be purchased. This includes a Philips head screwdriver.

HAND DRILLS

You will not go very far in modeling before you find the need for a hand drill. Older style hand drills from X-Acto came with a swivel head. The latest version of the hand drill has a solid head, and they have greatly improved the chucks for holding the drill bits. After using a swivel head drill for several years, I could not get accustomed to the fixed head. If you don't like the way the fixed hand drill feels after using it for a while, you might want to modify the drill.

The first step in converting the new drill to a swivel head is to remove the fixed wooden head. Do this with great care or you might split the head. I used a block of wood and a hammer to remove the head. Once the head is off, follow the steps shown in Figs. 2-2 and 2-3 to complete the conversion.

For larger drill bits, you will probably have to purchase a larger hand drill. The chucks in the X-Acto hand drill go to only #45. There will be times you will need to drill larger holes. Add these tools as they become necessary.

DRILL BITS

Hobby drill bits are fragile items and you will probably break your share until you get the feel of the drill. Take it easy when drilling and don't apply any side force on the bit while drilling or you will break the bit. All the words in the world won't mean anything here however, because only experience counts. Be resigned to the fact that you will be breaking the small bits until you acquire the knack of using the hand drill.

I suggest that you get a set of drill bits from #61 to #80. This way you will have the exact size bit you need for the job. Like any other tool, having

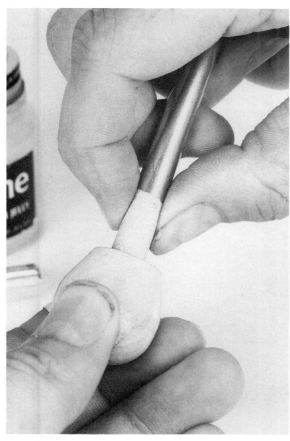

Fig. 2-3. Wrap a piece of sandpaper around the handle of a #1 X-Acto knife (remove the blade) and sand the wooden head enough so the head will swivel freely on the drill shaft. A little petroleum jelly on the shaft will make the head swivel easier.

the right one for the job at hand not only makes things go easier, but better too.

CLAMPS

You should have a few C-clamps on hand. The hardware store variety will serve most of your needs very well, and they are less costly. Many parts will need to be clamped together while the glue dries.

The best clamps are the ones you make yourself from simple spring-type clothespins (Fig. 2-4). The ends should be cut off and modified for easier use. The best thing about clothespins is that they are inexpensive and, if you have to modify one specifically for an unusual application, it matters little if you ever use the clothespin again. Clothespins are ideal for holding parts together while the glue dries or to hold parts for painting. Clothespins might well be your most versatile tool.

ADHESIVES

Unless you are building a snap-together kit, adhesives of some kind are needed to construct the model. Plastic glues come in tube or liquid form. For most times when plastic glue is needed, liquid glue should be used. Because tube glue is on the thick side, it is a little easier for final assemblies.

Never apply tube glue from the tube! Squeeze a little out on a file card—subscription cards from magazines work well for this—and apply the cement to the pieces to be joined. Use a toothpick or a straight pin. For gluing multi-piece assemblies together (engine blocks, seats rear ends, etc.) liquid glue is the best.

Epoxy

Although plastic glue can be used for the final assembly of a model car, epoxy is in many ways the best adhesive for finishing work. After trying several brands of epoxy, the one I always keep coming back to is Devcon 5-Minute Epoxy. Epoxy has many advantages over plastic glue in the final assembly stages, but it mainly adds to the speed of the final assembly. Many times, when you glue a fragile piece in place with plastic glue you must almost wait overnight for the joint to get a good bond so that you don't dislodge the part as you work on other areas of the model.

With epoxy, all you have to do is wait about five minutes before you can move on to the next assembly step. This is especially convenient if the chassis is a little sprung. If you had to hold the chassis in place until the glue dried, you might give up. Although waiting five minutes might seem like a long time, it is a lot better than actually holding the pieces in place for an hour or more.

If you get a spot of epoxy on a very visible area of your model, it can be removed easily. Accidents

Fig. 2-4. One of the cheapest tools you can get are simply spring type wood clothes pins. Modify the pins as shown in the photo to do many varied jobs. File a notch in the ends of the jaws for holding small round parts.

happen to the best and most careful of modelers. If the epoxy has not set yet, just wipe it off with a tissue. Make sure you get it all.

If the epoxy has set, as long as it hasn't set too long (perhaps overnight), you can still usually remove it with no damage to the car's finish. You can usually remove the drop of epoxy with the tip of your tweezers. In fact, many times I will apply enough epoxy to a part so it will ooze out on to the surface of the model. Once the epoxy has set, I carefully remove the excess epoxy. This will usually give you a very good bond.

Don't wait too long to remove the excess epoxy. If you let the epoxy set too long, it could take the paint with it when you try to remove it with your tweezers. Be especially careful with custom paints. If there is only a thin film of epoxy, the tweezers will not remove it. In this case, regular wax or Bare-Metal Plastic Polish can be used to remove the epoxy film—as long as it hasn't set up too hard. If it

has only been a few hours, you are fine. If it has been a few days, you might have problems.

Superglues

Cyanoacrylate adhesives provide a quick bond and have many time-saving applications in the model car field. Because these adhesives can bond skin to itself instantly, you should never get careless with these adhesives. After having tried many of the superglues, I keep coming back to one called Hot Stuff made by Satellite City. It is not only a good adhesive, it has the best applicator I have ever used. Satellite City makes superglues in a regular formula (Hot Stuff), and as a gap filling glue called Super T.

Although superglues are great for many applications where a strong bond is needed quickly, you should avoid using these adhesives on clear parts. Always read the manufacturers instructions on these products before using them.

ADVANCED TOOLS

As your building skills advance, you might want to add specialty tools to your collection. If there is a "must buy" advanced tool, it would have to be the Dremel Moto-Tool (Fig. 2-5). Dremel has many accessories to get the most out of the Moto-Tool. An accessory I recommend, if you plan to do any custom heat molding, is the Moto-Tool Speed Control. This is an almost must accessory for the Moto-Tool when you are working with plastic because the Moto-Tool is too fast for most plastic applications. For work with Auto World's AutoCutter (Fig. 2-6), the Speed Control can be used to lower the temperature so that it can be better used for heat molding.

LATHES AND MILLING MACHINES

After the Moto-Tool, a lathe and milling machine would just about complete the tool picture (Fig. 2-7). If you ever want to get into scratchbuilding, these two machines (sometimes combined in one machine) are a must for making the job easier. With these two machines, there is almost nothing you can't build, once you have acquired the necessary skills.

WORKBENCH

Ideally, all the tools you have should come together in the area of your workbench. It is the goal of almost all model car builders to have a permanent area for their workbench. In the long run, a permanent workbench will give you more time to spend on building model cars.

A fine model car can be built on a kitchen table, but be sure to protect the surface from scratches and spills if this is your work area. With this arrangement, however, you will be constantly picking up

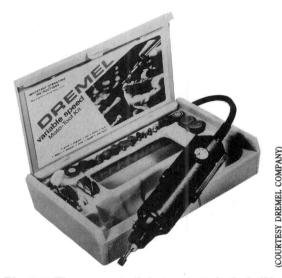

(COURTESY DREMEL COMPANY)

Fig. 2-5. There are not all that many tools the builder needs as they advance to a higher skill level, but the tools do become more expensive. One of the first tools the advanced builder should consider is the Dremel Moto-Tool with accessories.

Fig. 2-6. As your skills advance, a very useful tool is the Original Auto Cutter from Auto World. With this tool and its extra tips there are few operations you can't preform; especially useful to customizers.

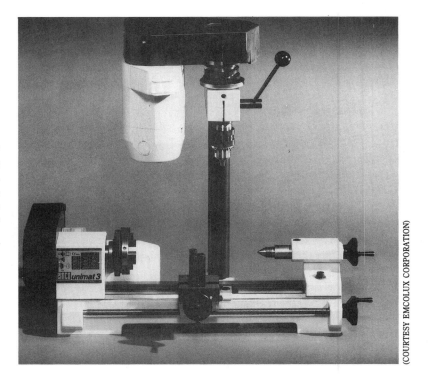

Fig. 2-7. The Unamat is a very versatile lathe/milling machine combination. With its many accessories, including wood working accessories, this small unit can do almost anything you could ever want to do in scratchbuilding.

what you are working on and setting up your tools again and again.

Obtaining furniture for a permanent workbench is usually no problem. It can be usually scrounged from a garage sale at a reasonable price. My workbench is an old dressing table with four drawers. As long as the basic unit is solid, the condition of the top does not matter. The top can be covered with a hard plastic top, or contact paper will work for a while.

Behind my bench is an old bookcase headboard with three compartments. One of these compartments holds my brush paints, the center is set up to hold my frequently used tools, and the other compartment is a catchall. Above the headboard, I built a shelf with sides so that it is free-standing on the

headboard. On the headboard, under the shelf, I have my parts cabinet. These cabinets store all kinds of small parts.

I also have several parts cabinets to hold the parts of the cars on which I am working. All kinds of tools and other assorted junk is on nails on the inside of the shelf. Above the shelf is a kit storage area. On one side of the bench there is a paper towel rack, and on the other side is a pegboard with my pliers and screwdrivers.

The other tools I use are stored in the drawers, along with other items like my sheet plastic. If possible, all the most used tools should be within easy reach. The more you can put in racks or holders, the better organized you will be. After any working session, return all of the tools to their proper places.

Chapter 3
Painting Model Cars

Before I get to the what and how of spray painting, there are a few general topics that should be covered. First, determine the area where you will be spray painting. Select as dry and dust free an area as you can find or make. If you select a basement for your spraying area, you should have a dehumidifier. I prefer painting where the humidity is 50 percent or less.

If you can create an area in your home where there is a minimum of dust, you will have no need to make a special spray booth. Few places are totally dust free, however. This is especially true after you start spray painting. Even if you don't need a spray booth to eliminate the dust from the paint, you should consider using a booth in order to keep the overspray off other items in the room.

SPRAY BOOTHS

If you are serious about building model cars and have the space to spare, you should consider making a permanent spray booth. The spray booth shown in Fig. 3-1 was made with a simple wood framework.

The framework was covered with sturdy cardboard and clear plastic. The actual box used to paint in is removable so that it can be thoroughly cleaned every now and then. This type of box should be cleaned a few hours before an important paint job.

This removable box was custom made to fit the framework. The area under the removable box was left open, with a flap made from clear plastic to allow entry to the booth. This keeps the dust out, but it is not the easiest way to enter a booth.

LIGHTING

Lighting is very important to obtain a good paint job. It is best to have one light in the booth and one light outside the booth. Keep the inside light on a few hours each day to help keep the booth dry. The best light for the outside of the booth is a reflector-type light.

VENTILATION

It is *very* important that you provide ventilation for the booth; otherwise, the fumes from the paint could

Fig. 3-1. If you intend to do a lot of spray painting, building a special spray booth is recommended.

injure or even kill you. In the removable box, I cut several holes and covered them with several layers of cheese cloth. To draw the fumes out of the booth, I hooked up an old vacuum cleaner (tank-type) to the booth, with the hose connected to a hole in the removable box. In the booth, there is a switch to turn the cleaner on to clear the air. There is also another switch for the compressor for the air brush.

Alternatives. If you are not going to be doing much painting, all you will really need is a large box to help catch the overspray and to help keep dust off the model until the paint dries in a few hours. If you have trouble with dust, tape a plastic drop cloth over the box and spray under the drop cloth.

If you live in an area with moderate temperatures, you might be able to set up a box outside to paint in on calm, dry days. That doesn't work in most places during the middle of January, but on a warm day, there are a number of smaller parts, such as interiors and frames, that you could paint out of doors.

ENAMEL PAINTS

Using any hobby spray paint isn't difficult once you learn how, but learning how to paint can be very frustrating. There are no easy steps to learn how to paint. It takes time and practice to develop the right touch to assure results that you can repeat. Learning how to operate a spray can will take longer than learning how to use tools.

Some people need more time to learn than others, but anyone can learn how to spray paint if he or she wants to. For the learning period, try to obtain some inexpensive model kits. If you do a poor job of painting, the paint can be soaked off (see Chapter 6), but it is best to have several spare models you can use for learning how to spray paint.

Before you start to paint, wash the part(s) in soapy water. This will remove any mold release that might still be on the parts. Rinse the washed parts with clean water and dry them before painting. If you have completely wet-sanded the body and parts, you can usually eliminate the washing step. Even then, it is best to wash the model before painting. When drying these parts after washing, do not rub them dry or you will build up static electricity, and the model will draw dust.

ATTACH PARTS FOR PAINTING

Wash your hands thoroughly before you attach parts to be painted to holders (Figs. 3-2 through 3-4). Avoid getting oily fingerprints on the model. In the painting area, wipe the model down with a tack rag to remove dust from the model.

Before painting, many hobbyists warm the paint cans slightly. Heat the cans in warm—but not hot—water. If the cans are heated too much, they will explode. Do not heat beyond the manufacturer's recommendation on the back of the can. Heating the paint cans seems to make the paint go on smoother.

CUSTOM PAINTS AND PRIMERS

Candy and metalflake paints need a base coat applied to the model before the color coats can be ap-

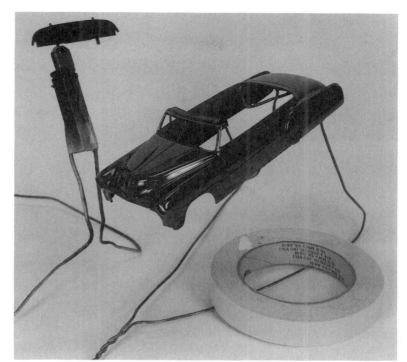

Fig. 3-2. Wire coat hangers bent to shape make the best holders, but holders such as toothpicks, paint-brush shafts and modified clothes pins all have their place in holding the parts while painting. On other items it is easier to epoxy them to a holder for painting. When the paint is dry, break the holder from the painted piece.

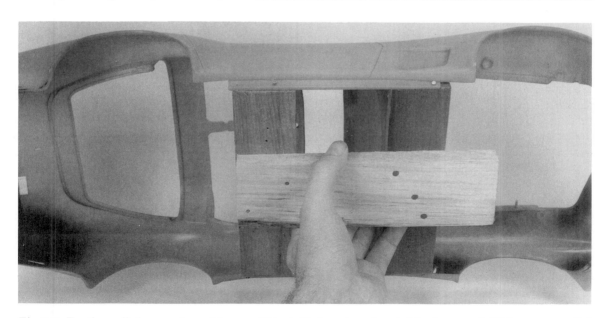

Fig. 3-3. For the really large scale models you will probably have to make a holder from wood. This one was nailed together with the model attached to the holder by drilling holes in the body (where they would be later covered by a chrome strip) and nailing the body to the holder. Great care is needed to remove the nails after the model is painted.

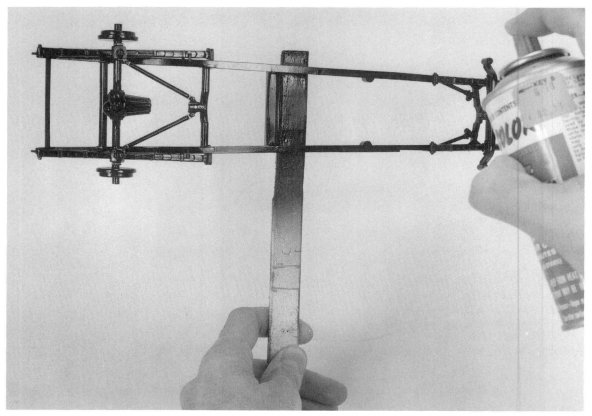

Fig. 3-4. Another method of holding piece to be painted is to bolt it to a strip of wood. It was especially easy in this case as that is the way this metal Duesenberg is set up. Use the hole pattern in the fender assembly to drill the holes in the wood.

plied. While you are learning to paint, avoid the custom colors. Unless you have done some custom work to the body or applied putty that needs to be primed, in most cases you will not need to apply a primer. In learning to paint, the less preparation there is before you start applying the color coats the better.

With this out of the way, you should be ready to actually try your hand at painting.

First wipe the model with a tack rag to remove any dust. Heat the spray can as described above. Spray on the first coat in a light mist from 10″ to 12″ from the car. This coat should be applied in a quick motion so that you just get a light dusting of paint on the model.

Dust on a couple of coats from the 10″ to 12″ range (Fig. 3-5), allowing each coat to dry briefly before applying the next. Move in a little closer and apply one or two more coats. At this stage the model should be uniformly covered. At the end of this stage, all wheel openings and hood openings and door openings should have enough paint on them so that you don't have to make a special effort to paint them again.

Now move in a little closer with the can and apply the final "color coat." The secret here is to have a good light over your shoulder. Work the car into position so that while you are spraying the color coat the light is shining on the area you are painting. With the light just right, you will be able to see when you

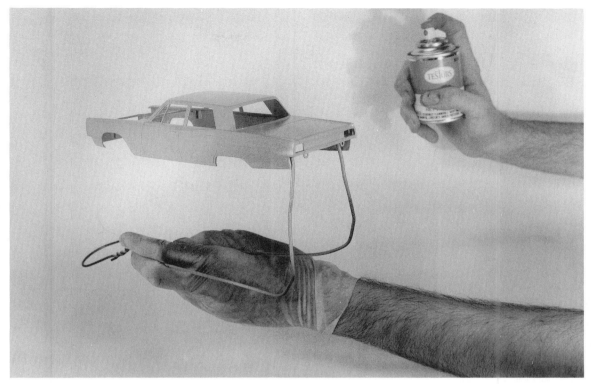

Fig. 3-5. The distance of the spray can from the model and the speed of passes across the model determine the final appearance of paint application.

have applied just enough paint to give the model a smooth glossy appearance, but not so much paint it will run (Fig. 3-6).

If you don't get it right the first time, just keep on trying. Learning to paint isn't all that difficult; it just takes practice to assure consistency (Fig. 3-7).

Problems and Solutions

If you are not careful when applying the paint, runs and sags are likely. These problems occur when you apply too much paint to the surface, and it has no place else to go but down. Thank you gravity! The results are runs or sags. Once this happens, there is little you can do except strip the paint and start over.

If you want to make an attempt at salvaging the paint job, hold the model so that the paint run is horizontal. Keep turning the model to keep the paint from settling too heavily in any one area. By keeping the model moving, you might be able to get the paint run to flatten out. Do this until the paint is dry enough so it won't run any more. By keeping the run area basically horizontal but moving, you can sometimes salvage a ruined paint job. If any more paint needs to be applied after this, wait a couple of days to let everything dry before applying the final coats.

The reason for runs and sags is too much paint applied too quickly. Correct this by either moving the can farther from the model before you start to spray or by moving the can across the model (while spraying) faster. Either way will result in less paint on the model at any one time and eliminate the possibility of runs or sags.

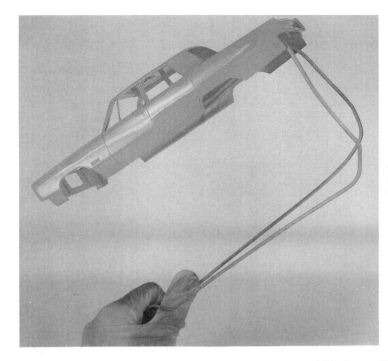

Fig. 3-6. Proper lighting is essential when checking paint for proper thickness.

Lighting

If you have a good light over your left shoulder (if you are right-handed) or your right shoulder (if you are left-handed), you can hold the model car so that you can see when you have applied just enough paint. Position the model so that the light is shining on the area you are painting. With a little practice, you can tell when you have applied just enough paint. You can see the paint go on and become very smooth and glossy. If you apply just a little more paint to the area, you will have runs. One secret of good painting is to get the light in the right area while you apply just the right amount of paint to produce a high gloss. Practice until you know how much paint is enough. Really, this sounds a lot harder than it actually is.

Orange Peel

Orange peel paint looks just like the name implies. The surface of the model looks just like the surface of an orange. A frequent problem here is that the paint is too dry when it hits the surface of the model.

This is usually caused by having the spray can too far from the model or moving the can across the model too quickly. The solution is to move in closer when spraying or to slow down the motion of your pass. All paint will have an orange peel look until the final color coat.

Bubbles in the Paint

A bad can of paint can cause bubbles in the paint, but that is seldom the case. Like everything else, paint manufacturers can't be perfect 100 percent of the time. Another cause of bubbles in the paint is spraying too close to the model. Move back a bit when spraying. High humidity can also cause bubbles. In this case, all you can do is wait for the humidity to drop before painting again. Another problem associated with high humidity is *blushing* of the paint. With this problem, the paint takes on a cloudy look. This can sometimes be corrected by applying heat to the model. You have to be careful, however, because too much heat could warp the plastic.

Custom Paints

Candy and metalflake paints need a special base coat before you can apply the color coat. The most popular base colors are metallic silver, gold, or copper but any solid color can be used as a base for an interesting effect. After the base is applied, allow it to dry before starting with the custom colors.

It is very hard to match up various body pieces with custom colors. Every coat you apply changes the overall tone of the color. Whenever possible, tape all of the body pieces together and paint them as a unit. The base can and should be applied to the individual body pieces before you tape them in place.

When you have a model with doors that open, painting the body as a one-piece unit is just not possible. Your best bet is to paint this type of model in solid colors. They are easier to match up, and the parts can be painted separately. If you must paint a model with opening doors in a candy color, there is something you can at least try. After the base is applied, paint only the door jambs on the body and the doors themselves.

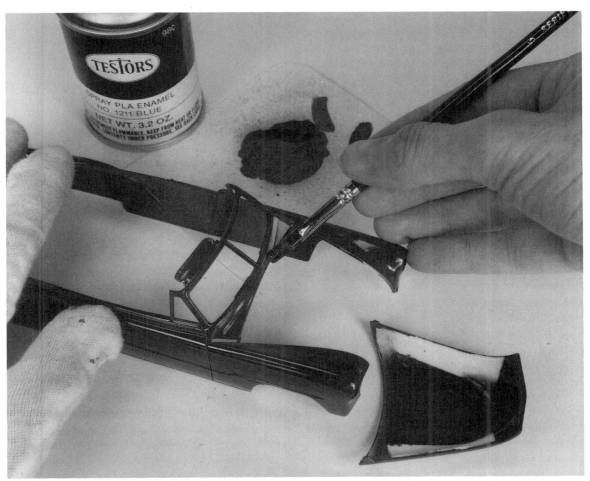

Fig. 3-7. When the paint is dry, remove any parts you taped in place. Touch up the areas on items like the hood cover using the same paint used to paint the body (if any is left). Spray the paint on a file card and brush it on as shown.

Let this paint become totally dry. Now you can tape the doors in place and paint the body as a unit. Do your best to try to blend the color where it is darker around the door areas because of the overspray from the jambs. This is difficult, but it is about the only way to paint custom colors and get a perfect match between the body parts.

Drying Time

Enamel paints are slow to dry. It is best to allow a minimum of at least three days drying time for enamel-painted cars before starting the final assembly. A week's drying time is preferable. Even after a week, the painted surface should be handled no more than is necessary. Handle the model with cotton gloves.

The drying time can be decreased if you put the parts under a heat source. The use of only moderate heat cannot be stressed enough. Too high a heat will not only ruin the paint, but could damage the plastic as well. The heat from an ordinary electric bulb is usually more than enough to warm the parts to help speed drying. Remember to keep checking the heat you are applying to the parts.

WAX FOR ENAMEL PAINTS

Once the paint has dried, you might want to apply a coat of wax to the model. You must be careful here because some automotive waxes can ruin enamel paint. One wax that can be used with enamel is Turtle Extra Wax. Do not apply the wax as stated on the package. If you apply the wax and allow it to dry, you might never get it off the paint.

Apply the wax almost as if it were a rubbing compound. (Refer to the next section of this chapter for tips in this area.) Rub the wax on the model with a soft cloth (cotton is best). Rub in a circular motion whenever possible. The rag will probably discolor as it would with rubbing compound.

Work a small area at a time, and before the wax has a chance to dry, rub it off with a clean soft cloth or unscented tissue. With a little buffing, the paint should take on a very high shine. Before starting, allow at least a week's drying time (longer is preferable). Before starting on the complete model, test

the wax out on a part of the model that isn't as easily seen—a lower quarter panel rather than the hood or trunk. Be sure that the wax doesn't damage the paint.

AUTOMOTIVE PAINTS

If you were to spray an automotive paint directly on a plastic model car, the solvents in the paint would attack the plastic. This would cause a condition known as *crazing*. Crazing results from the solvents melting the surface of the plastic and causing it to wrinkle. On some parts, like interiors, this isn't all bad, because it simulates a textured surface. But on the surface of a body, that texture is definitely not wanted.

If you are making authentic replica stock models, painting them in the proper color is a very desirable option and the preferable way to go. The best known of the automotive touch-up paints are those from Dupli-Color and Plastic-Kote. In order to be able to apply these automotive paints to a plastic model, the model must first be sealed so that the color coat won't craze the plastic body.

There are a number of fine primers available that will protect the plastic (Fig. 3-8). After trying several types, my preference is the one made by Tempo: #7-4000 Platinum Gray Sandable Primer. It is a very good general-use primer even if you plan on painting enamels. The primer is applied in the same manner you would apply any paint. Being an automotive paint, it dries much faster than enamels. Therefore, it is less likely to run. When the primer is dry, it must be sanded smooth. When sanding the primer down, take care to make sure you do not sand completely through the primer. If you do, prime the area you sanded through and be more careful as you sand the primed area smooth again.

Even though the automotive primer does dry quickly, it is best to let it dry overnight before sanding it down. The harder the primer is, the better protection it will give the plastic. With the primer sanded down, you are ready to spray on the color coat.

Dusting on the first few color coats is especially important when you are using automotive paints over

Fig. 3-8. When mixing primer for spraying, mix it about one part primer and six to eight times that amount of thinner. To assure consistency in the mix, select a small jar and mark it off so you will know how much primer you need and how much thinner.

plastic. If you apply the paint too thickly, it might not run, but it could dry slow enough so that solvents will soften the primer and cause crazing. It would be best if you gradually built up the color coat and then let the body dry for at least a few hours before applying the final coat. Don't apply the paint too heavily. Just because the paint doesn't run doesn't mean you aren't applying it too heavily. Automotive paints do not run as easily as hobby paints. Therefore, applying them too thickly is easier to do. If you apply an automotive paint too thickly, even with the best of primer, the plastic is likely to craze.

Once the color coat has dried, you will have to rub out the paint to get a high gloss. After the au-

tomotive paint has dried, it will look like orange peel; this is normal.

In my experience with automotive paints, I have found that metallic paints give the best results. They are less likely to craze the plastic than solid colors. I would also like to stress the importance of testing the paint out on each model before you actually paint the model. The kit you have selected will probably have some accessory part that can be used for the test. It is always best to use a piece from the actual kit for the test because all styrene plastic is not the same. Some craze easier than others, and you never know which ones will craze until you start to paint. Paint the test piece exactly as you would the body. If there is any tendency to craze, switch primers and try again on another piece of test plastic.

A good example of the need to test each car you are painting is the kits that were produced in the mid-1970s, during the first energy shortage scare. Because of the shortage of oil, plastics were getting hard to come by. To keep the kits in production, AMT used some extenders in their plastic. These kits have a very milky, semi-transparent look to them. Painting these kits with regular enamel paint is no problem, but some automotive paints I tried crazed badly. Even the primer crazed one of these cars, so you really have to be careful when you are working with automotive paints.

Alternatives. While at least one brand of the automotive touch-up paint is available almost everywhere, the primer might be a little more difficult to come by. Tempo's primer is the best in my book, but others will work as well. Plasti-Kote makes a good white primer (#636). And though I haven't tried it, I have read that Martin-Senour makes a good primer as well (#7865). It is available at NAPA dealers. I have also heard Tempo makes another primer (#611) that works well with plastic model cars. Not having used the last two products, I cannot say for sure that they will work well over plastic models, but I do trust the sources from whom I received the tips. I am also sure that there are other primers that would work well. If you can't find the primers I have mentioned, try some of the primers that are available to you. Be sure to thoroughly test them before spraying an important model.

AIR BRUSHES

Don't let anyone tell you that an air brush is a must if you are going to be a serious model car builder. It just isn't true. I have used an air brush for a while now and still prefer a spray can when I can use one. There comes a time, however, when the limitations of colors and of spraying techniques as well as control make an air brush a needed investment.

Air brushes come in all styles and price ranges. After having used inexpensive units and costly units, I can say that both have their advantages. If you are on a small budget, your best bet is to purchase one of the inexpensive Badger units. This will set you back very little and will get you started in air brush painting.

The only negative aspect of an inexpensive unit is that it isn't very versatile. It doesn't have the spray pattern control of an expensive unit. If your reason for wanting an air brush is the unlimited adjustments available, then you should consider an expensive unit. If you think you will have to spray into confined areas, then an expensive brush should be your first consideration. After using both inexpensive and expensive air brushes, I would hate to be without either. The inexpensive brush has a much wider spray pattern that is ideal for larger scale models or the quick application of primer.

Air Supply for Air Brushes

To operate an air brush, you need a source of compressed air. There are several ways you can deliver the air to the air brush. The best route is also the most expensive, but, in the long run, a compressor and a holding tank will be your best investment if you are serious about air brushing. The tank is filled with air and you paint using the reserve air, with the compressor off most of the time. In this way, you will not have a loud compressor going while you are painting. These are very expensive units.

If a compressor is out of your budget range, a good alternative is a can of compressed air. Badger's Propel cans are remarkably long lasting. I recommend the large economy size. Cans of compressed air do have their problems. As the cans get low on air, they tend to lose pressure quickly. Also, if you are spraying for a long time, the cans tend to get very cool. This also tends to make them lose pressure. To counter this, always have several cans on hand.

Paints and Thinners

The biggest advantage of an air brush is that you can use any type of paint in them. Both Testor and Pactra jar paints can be used in most air brushes—although the pigment of some of the paints will not go though some air brushes—and they make a lot more colors in brush jars than in spray cans. Most paint thinners can be used with these hobby enamels.

Automotive paints are also easy to apply with an air brush. Dupli-Color 1-ounce jars are ideal, but they are not available everywhere. If you can't find these jars, you have little choice but to obtain the paints you want in pints. And that will paint a lot of model cars! If pints are the only way you can get the paints you want, you might be able to trade some to friends. You also might be able to obtain small quantities of paint from a body shop. They often have small amounts of paint left over and might be willing to help you out. Explain to them why you want the paint and take a couple of the cars you have built along to give them an idea of why you want the paint.

The best primer I have found for air brush use is DuPont's 30S Platinum Gray High Speed Lacquer Type Primer Surfacer. When it is thinned properly, this is an excellent all-purpose primer. I also recommend DuPont's Y-3613S Lo Temp Non-Penetrating Acrylic Lacquer Thinner. The smallest quantity you can get is a quart of primer and a gallon of thinner. These amounts are not excessive. If you get into air brushing automotive paints, you will be buying more before you know it.

MIXING AND APPLYING PRIMER

Consistency is very important in the primer. You will likely have to do some experimenting to come up with the best working ratio between primer and thinner. Once you get the best ratio, mark the jar so that you can duplicate the results the next time.

Transferring the primer from the can to the jar can be a problem. Before you do start, shake the can and make sure the primer is well mixed. Pry the lid open. Because of the small quantity of paint involved, one of the best ways to transfer the paint from the can to the mixing jar is to dip a screwdriver in the primer and let it run off into the jar. This is messy, but so is any other method. Because the primer is on the thick side, you could also scoop up some on a file card and transfer it this way. Wipe the screwdriver off after use.

Working with a gallon of thinner isn't easy when you only need a small amount at a time. Transfer some of the thinner to a smaller container (a pint is about right) and get the thinner you need for mix-ing paint from this. An eye dropper works well for transferring thinner to the mixing jar.

Once the primer and the thinner are in the mixing jar, shake the jar until the two are completely mixed. You might want to hold back a little thinner to really get all the primer out of the mixing jar. Once the primer and thinner are mixed, pour this into the painting jar (straining it first). Then pour a little more thinner into the mixing jar, shake it up and pour the remainder in the painting jar. This way you will get all the primer out of the mixing jar.

Although painting with an air brush is similar to painting with a spray can, the big difference is that with an air brush you can move in a lot closer to the body. How close depends on the air brush you are using. Apply the primer pretty much as you would any paint. Sand it smooth when it is dry (Fig. 3-9).

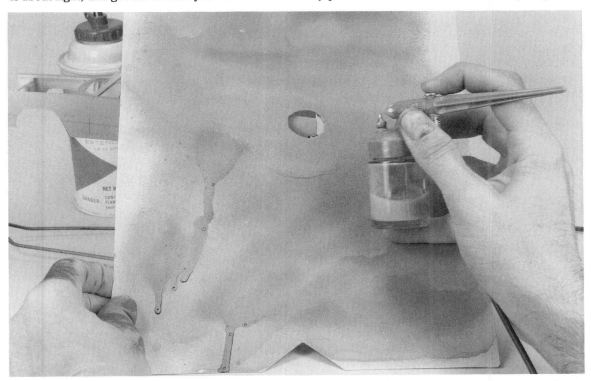

Fig. 3-9. Once the primer is dry, sand it down. If you sand through the primer, cut a hole in a piece of cardboard. Position the hole in the cardboard over the area that needs more primer. Apply the primer to the necessary area. The hole will allow the primer to reach the area that needs paint, but the rest of the cardboard will keep the over-spray off the model you have already sanded. This method can also be used with spray cans and for color coats with lacquer paints.

MIXING A COLOR COAT

There can be no set formula for mixing the color coat. Some paints will be on the thin side as they come from the jar or can. Use less thinner to thin these to painting consistency. Naturally, you must do the opposite with paint that seems thicker than normal. Whatever you do, don't thin all the paint you have at one time. Put some aside in case you thin the paint too much.

Only experience can be your guide in mixing the paint. If you are unsure of the proper mixture, lean toward the thin side and add more unthinned paint if necessary.

I suggest using separate mixing jars for primers, mixing solid colors, and mixing metallic colors. For the air brush, I suggest having separate color jars for the solid colors and metallics. The reason for this is simple. Even if you clean the color or mixing jars well, there is always the possibility of some contamination when you switch from using metallic paints to using solids. For the price of the jars, it is a wise investment. After using metallics, always be sure to clean the air brush very carefully (Fig. 3-10).

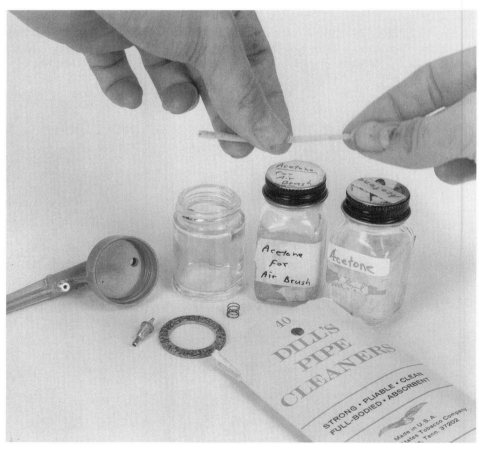

Fig. 3-10. After painting with an air brush you must clean the brush completely. The paint jar must be especially clean or you could ruin the next model you try to paint. The quickest way to clean these parts is with acetone, but use acetone with extreme caution. Regular lacquer thinners can also be used, but they take longer. The metal parts of the air brush can be soaked in acetone for a thorough cleaning.

RUBBING OUT THE PAINT

To get a really smooth finish with automotive paints, they must be rubbed out. Rubbing compound comes in many styles and grades of coarseness (Fig. 3-11). For most model car work, a liquid rubbing compound will work very well. Liquid rubbing compounds, along with polishing compounds made for the model car hobby, are available from several manufacturers. When working with an automotive compound, you should test it before using it on a prize model, just to make sure it is not too coarse for use on a model car. On stubborn cases with much orange peel, you might have to resort to a paste rubbing compound that is a little more coarse. You could also sand the surface down slightly with very used 600-grit wet sandpaper, but don't sand too much or you might sand through the finish.

Apply a bit of the compound to a piece of soft cloth (cotton is preferable). Whenever possible, rub the model in a circular motion in a random pattern. For most areas of the body, you can apply pressure to the model while rubbing with your index finger. Don't use too much pressure, because it will increase the depth of the scratches. There will be some areas of the body you will not be able to reach with your finger. For these areas, you will have to wrap the cloth around something else to finish rubbing out the body. A flat toothpick will usually work well.

After you have been rubbing for a while, wipe the excess compound off and buff the area with a clean cloth or unscented tissue. Do not continue rubbing if the compound appears dry; wipe it off. Keep applying compound and checking the surface frequently. Stop when the surface is smooth. Be careful not to rub through the paint. Special care must be taken when you rub around door lines, raised edges, or corners. It is very easy to rub through

Fig. 3-11. With automotive paint of any kind, you will have to rub the finish out to get a perfectly smooth job. For most model work, liquid rubbing compounds are best.

these areas. Edges and ridges have the least amount of paint on them to begin with, so be extra careful when you work around these areas.

RETOUCHING THIN AREAS

If you should rub through automotive paints, correcting the problem is relatively easy. The steps used to describe touching up primer (Fig. 3-8) apply equally for touching up a color coat. After a little rubbing with a liquid rubbing compound, however, you should lightly sand the area you are going to retouch. Use 600-grit paper. The paint doesn't stick too well to a highly polished surface. Generally, you should be able to paint over an area you rubbed out with compound, but again, you may want to make some tests on painted scrap plastic first. You should be able to paint over compound, but you can't paint over a surface that has been waxed without first removing that wax.

Regular rubbing compounds, even liquid ones, are sometimes a bit too coarse, leaving fine scratches in the paint. Although this may not be noticeable on a real car, it will be noticeable on a model. Finish rubbing with fine polish is recommended, because this should take the finish to a mirror sheen, without the noticeable scratches.

COMPOUND CLEAN UP

When you have finished rubbing the body out to a smooth finish, you will probably have excess compound in all the door lines and any other body recesses. File the end of a flat toothpick so that it is narrow enough to get in the door lines. Use this modified toothpick to clean the compound from the door lines and anywhere else it might have accumulated. In some cases, you might have to wrap a piece of cloth around the toothpick to remove all of the compound. You must remove all the excess compound to obtain a finished look to the model.

FINAL TOUCH UP AND WAX

Some areas you have rubbed through might not need to be touched up with spray paint. If the area is small and not in a noticeable place, you might be able to touch it up with a paintbrush. Work quickly with the paintbrush because automotive paints dry rapidly.

The final step in finishing a model is the wax job. It is usually easiest to apply the wax after final assembly. In some cases, waxing before final assembly is necessary if the finished model has any places that are hard to reach. A good wax job will usually hide any small scratches left by rubbing out the model. It is, however, almost impossible to completely remove all of the scratches.

TWO-TONE PAINTING

Two-tone paint jobs for model cars are just starting to come into favor after years of single-tone paint jobs. In the '50s, two-tone (and even three-tone) paint jobs were common on cars. For the most part, two-tone paint jobs are not hard to do, but they do take a lot more time to complete.

Masking Off the Body

In the long run, if there is a natural body line—either a chrome trim strip or a natural sharp dividing line to the body—you will save time by masking off the area of the body that will be getting the second color (Figs. 3-12 and 3-13). By doing this, you will eliminate having to sand down the overspray from the first color before you apply the second color. Although you do have to mask the model twice this way, you do save time because it is sometimes difficult to sand the overspray from the first color. There are times when you might be able to paint the complete body with the first color and then just spray the second color over the first. This does make for a rather thick coat of paint; if there are any detail moldings under the area of the second color, they could be lost with the two full coats of paint over them. With cars like the Monogram Corvette, there are no natural body lines and no choice but to deal with the overspray. Make sure that the first color covers all the necessary areas if you don't paint the complete body in the first color.

Another problem for cars without natural body line is masking off for the second color. In cases like this, it is especially important to paint the lighter color on first. With the first color completely dry, the masking can start for the second color.

Fig. 3-12. If the body has a natural dividing line, use them as a guide to mask off the first color you painted. On models such as the Monogram Corvette with no molding, it is easiest to just spray the area with the first color, let it dry and then sand the overspray down where the second coat will be.

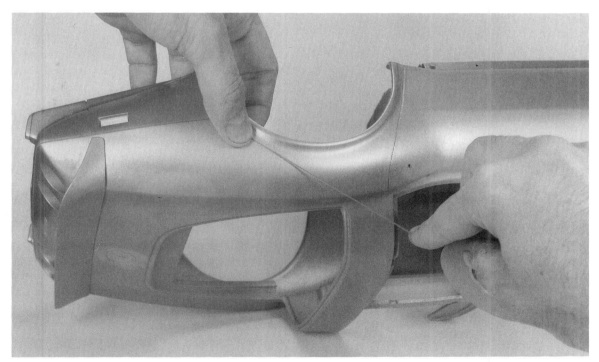

Fig. 3-13. On cars without a natural body line to mask against, a makeshift one can be made by applying 1/32-inch pin striping tape.

The solution to the problem of no body line is something called Chartpack $\frac{1}{32}$-inch crepe pin striping tape. Crepe tape is recommended, because it will take a curve and regular pinstriping tape will not. To get the tape to go around a curved area, lead the tape by several inches. Carefully guide the tape into position and press it in contact with the body using your finger. This will be your guide for cutting the masking. Make sure that this tape is applied accurately. If you are not making any curves, you do not need to apply the tape to make a guide for cutting the masking. A straightedge will work, and it will save you a lot of trouble.

Bare-Metal Foil is used as the masking medium (Fig. 3-14). Refer to Chapter 4 for full information on how to apply the foil. The first step is to apply a small piece of foil to each door seam and any other natural body seams the paint line will cross. If you don't do this, the paint might seep down the cracks and ruin the paint job. Next, apply strips of foil around the body using the pin striping tape as a guide.

With the foil in place, but not yet in firm contact with the body, mask off the rest of the body with regular masking tape and paper. Be careful while applying the masking tape because it could cause the foil to lift. The masking tape and paper should completely cover the area you painted first.

With the first color completely covered, use a toothpick to get the Bare-Metal Foil in firm contact with the body and up against the tape dividing line (Fig. 3-15). With the foil in firm contact with the body, you can start trimming the foil. Trimming the foil on a body with a molded-in body line of some kind is a snap. With the pin striping tape guide line, you must be very careful while cutting the foil. Take your time as you trim the foil. A slip now could mean starting all over. When the foil is trimmed, remove

Fig. 3-14. Apply strips of Bare-Metal Foil to the areas to be masked off. Treat the taped line the same way you would a natural body molding. Using masking tape and paper, mask off the rest of the area you want to protect. Leave no spots uncovered or overspray will find them.

the excess foil and the pin striping tape from the body. (Refer to Fig. 3-16.) Spray on the second color. The first few coats of this second color should be applied very lightly to help eliminate any possibility of the second color bleeding under the masking to the first color.

Removing the Masking

When you have a natural body line separating the two colors, before you remove the masking, cut through the paint using a sharp X-Acto knife with a #11 blade. This will give you a sharper color dividing line and make removing the masking easier. It will also eliminate any chance that you will chip the paint when you remove the masking. If you can't cut through the paint before you remove the masking, remove the masking as soon as possible (Fig. 3-17). This is especially true with automotive paints.

Take great care in how you handle the model while removing the masking. The paint will not have had a chance to dry if you are working on a model like the Corvette.

Spray-On Masking

Spray-on maskers show a lot of promise (Fig. 3-18). There have been brush-on maskers available for a long time, but the ones I have tried in the past never seemed to work well for me. The Metalflake Spray Mask I used for this chapter can also be brushed on, but spraying is the best method. Again, experiment on test models before taking a chance on damaging a model you have worked on for a long time. This spray-on masker will go over bare plastic with no problem. (Almost nothing will mask candy enamel paints, no matter how they are applied.)

Fig. 3-15. With the first color masked off, trim the Bare-Metal Foil using the striping tape as a guide line. Remove the excess foil and striping tape and clean up any tape residue. Make sure that the remaining Bare-Metal is in firm contact with the body. Go over it with a flat toothpick to be sure.

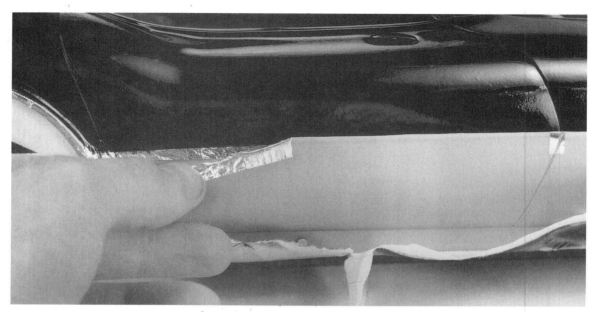

Fig. 3-16. Spray on the second coat of paint. As soon as possible (especially with automotive paints), remove the foil masker. Remove the masking tape first then peel off the foil over itself as shown.

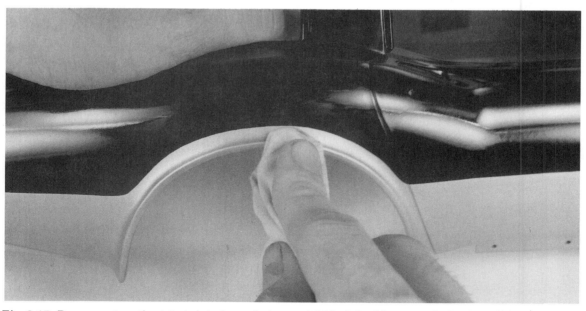

Fig. 3-17. Because automotive type paints dry so fast you might be left with a ragged edge for a parting line. Go over the line with rubbing compound that is applied to a piece of cloth wrapped around something like the rounded end of a ruler. By working carefully and as soon as the paint can be handled, you should be able to clean the line up considerably.

42

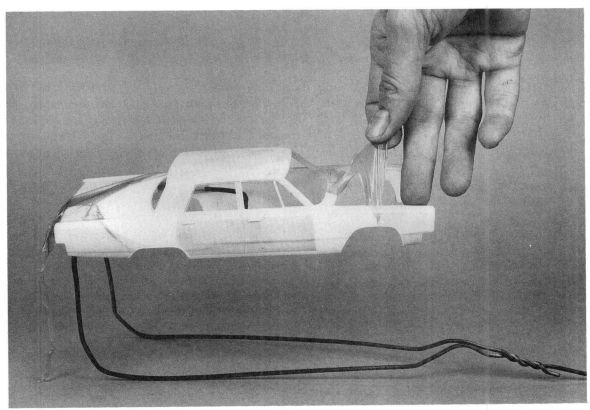

Fig. 3-18. Spray maskers offer a lot of promise in two tone painting. Simply spray the masker over the entire car as described on the package and let it dry for the recommended time. Then using a #1 X-Acto knife, cut around the area you want to remain the original color. You can now lift the masking from the areas of the model body that you want to paint.

I would also suggest trying spray-on masking for the area that will receive the second color. It is a good idea to cut through the paint, if possible, using the same techniques as with regular masking. As with the regular masking, I believe this would help eliminate any possibility of the paint chipping when you remove the spray-on masker.

When spraying masker on, do so in several heavy coats. Apply this masker heavily. If you put it on too thinly, it is impossible to get off. And half the fun is in removing the masker!

Chapter 4

Building and
Detailing Model Cars

Now that you have had a look at the basic areas of model building, it is time to start building a model car. If you are looking for a hobby, model cars is one of the easiest hobbies to start. The reason for this is the current state of the snap-together model car kit.

Most of the snap kits on the market today have wide appeal, because they are very well detailed, and they are accurate models of real cars. Snap kits are ideal for the beginning model car builder. They can be completed in a very short time, and maintaining interest in a hobby is easy when the first few models can be completed quickly. Progress must be made, or the starting modeler could lose interest. Snap kits are also ideal for the model car buff who is just too busy to put several hundred hours into a model.

QUICK ASSEMBLY

Just assembled out of the box, the modern snap kit provides an accurate model that is molded in an attractive color. There is very little work involved.

With just a little more detailing, however, you can have an individual piece that is an even greater source of pride. The model used as an example in this part of the chapter is the Jo-Han Cadillac Coupe DeVille Coupe (CS-505). Please note: the kit used to illustrate these tips (and the kits used throughout this book) is being used only to demonstrate the tips; any similar model can be used. The same applies to the paint—Humbrol was used because I had it on hand and I like it. All tips are only suggestions, and what works well for one builder may not work at all for another. Test products out and use what works best for you. In order to detail the completed model as shown in Fig. 4-1, you would need the following items:

☐ Jo-Han Cadillac Coupe DeVille kit.
☐ X-Acto #1 knife (comes with #11 blade).
☐ Grumbacher #7701 brush ¼-inch wide (wide flat brush).
☐ Humbrol HM11 tin of black paint (flat).
☐ Humbrol HM9 tin scarlet paint (flat).
☐ Thinner and jar to clean brushes.

Fig. 4-1. Though the finished model took very little time to complete, the addition of a few painted features made this simple snap-together kit something special.

Because it is a snap kit, you might question the need for an X-Acto knife. I would like to make a very important point. You should *never* break a part from the plastic runner (also known as a *tree* or a *sprue*). If you break the part off the runner, there is a strong possibility you will leave a bit of the part on the runner. Needless to say, that could ruin the looks of the finished model. All parts should always be cut, or in some cases sawed, off the runners. There are few exceptions to this.

You might also question using Humbrol scarlet to paint the interior if the interior of the Jo-Han Cadillac Coupe DeVille is already molded in red. The reason is that plastic left unpainted has too much of a shine for areas like the interior, which should be nearly a flat color. The interior was painted because that is the way I wanted it. If you prefer to leave it or paint it another color, that is up to you. Always build the model to please yourself. You are the one who will be living with the finished product.

MORE DETAILING

To gain experience in building model cars, you might want to build a few snap kits right out of the box and add nothing to them. Then you could work up to the detailing shown in Figs. 4-2 through 4-6. If you still don't feel confident enough to move on, you can still get a lot more out of a snap kit.

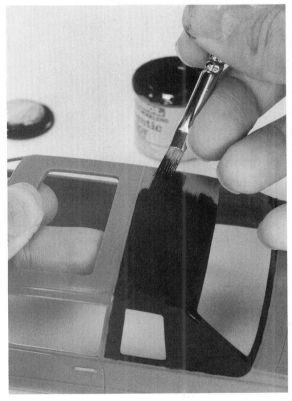

Fig. 4-2. When painting a vinyl roof, be careful not to get any paint on the body; don't worry about getting paint on the chrome trim molding.

First you could rub out the body with rubbing compound or a plastic polish. That is all that is necessary, and it usually gives a very high gloss to plastic. You could even go one step further. Sand down the mold parting lines (described in the next section of this chapter) with 400-grit wet sandpaper and follow this with the used 600-grit wet sandpaper. This will remove the mold lines and leave the body

Fig. 4-3. After you finish painting the black vinyl top, paint the chassis black next. If axles are plastic, paint them black as well.

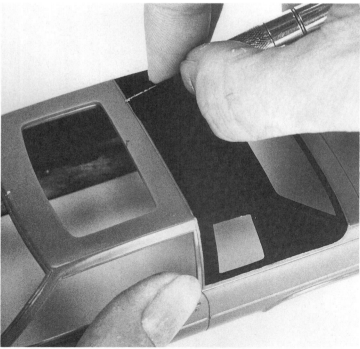

Fig. 4-4. When the paint on the roof is dry, scrape off any paint you may have gotten on the trim molding. Take care you don't scratch the body.

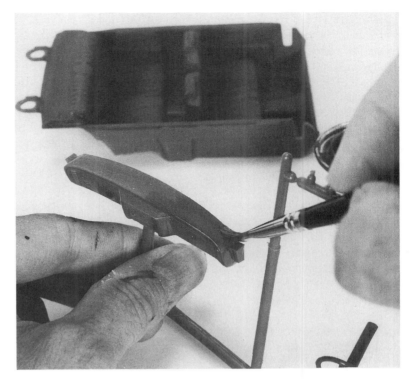

Fig. 4-5. While painting the interior parts, leave items like the instrument panel, steering wheel, seats, etc., attached to plastic runners. They are easier to paint this way. After paint is dry, cut them from the runners and touch up the spot where they were attached.

rather scratched. Next, rub the areas you sanded with a liquid rubbing compound to remove the deeper scratches. Follow this rubbing compound with a plastic polish to completely remove the scratches and bring the plastic to a high sheen. When you are finished, you should not be able to tell where the mold parting lines were.

To add the ultimate amount of realism, you could detail the chrome trim with Bare-Metal Foil as described in the next section. Detailed in this manner, your simple snap kit will look just as detailed as a regular model car kit.

Some snap kits even come with engines, so just a little detailing to the body will allow you to easily come up with a fairly impressive model car—even if it is the first model car you build. Snap kits are NOT just for the young modeler, and they can be a lot of fun to build.

THE BASIC KIT

Once you get your feet wet with a few snap kits, you will probably want to expand your skills to regu-

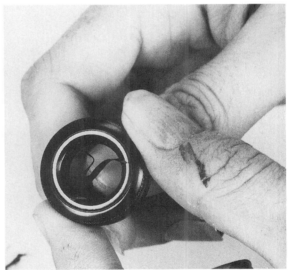

Fig. 4-6. If the tires on the snap kit are a little too tight to fit on the wheels, you might have to trim a bit of the tire where it contacts the wheel. Don't remove too much, or the wheel will be too loose and need to be epoxied in place.

lar model car kits. If you do, painting is the next skill you should learn. With so many of the kits being molded in color, however, even this is not a skill needed right away anymore. For the following example, the 1951 Chevrolet convertible from AMT was used.

The first step before you can start painting the model is to remove the mold parting lines (Fig. 4-7). All model kits have parting lines. Molds are not one piece, and where two parts of the mold come together, there is a mold line. No matter how well the parts of the mold fit, there will be mold parting lines.

Sand down the mold lines first with 400-grit wet sandpaper (Fig. 4-8). Now check the body for sink marks (Fig. 4-9). Sink marks, slight dips or depressions in the body, are not present on all model kits, but they are common. Sink marks show up on the surface of the body where the plastic is thick. Be-

fore painting, these should be filled in so that the body is smooth.

APPLYING BODY PUTTY

After trying many types of body putty, I started using a 3M product called Acryl-Red Body Putty. When I couldn't find the Acryl-Red when I needed a new tube, I tried another 3M putty, Acryl-Blue, which is every bit as good as Acryl-Red. This is a true automotive body putty, and it is better than any hobby putty I know of by a wide margin. Like any putty, you should never apply a heavy coat. If the area needs to be built up, do it in several thin layers. Also, the solvents in the putty might attack the plastic if it is applied too thickly. Acryl-Red putty can usually be sanded after about 30 minutes. If it is a little thicker than it should be, however, it will take longer to dry. Allow ample drying time. Acryl-Red

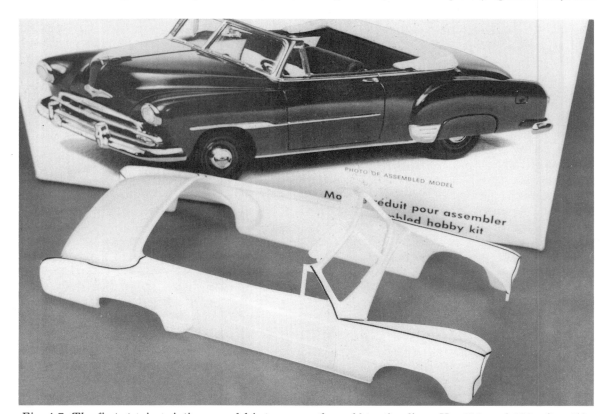

Fig. 4-7. The first step in painting a model is to remove the mold parting lines. Use 400- and 600-grit wet/dry sandpaper—used wet here. Mold parting lines on this kit are outlined in black tape.

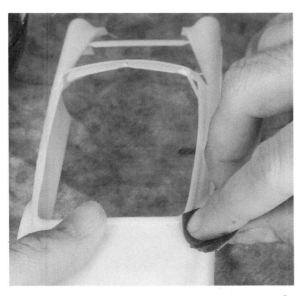

Fig. 4-8. To get the mold parting lines sanded out right up to the molded-in chrome detailing, use your fingernail to get the sandpaper in close. Be careful not to sand away any detail.

will bond to the plastic body and fill even tiny pin holes. The only other putty I know of that ever came close to being better than Acryl-Red is one called Quicksilver Plastic Putty made by Krasel Industries. Unfortunately, Quicksilver had shelf life problems and hasn't been available for several years.

Sand the putty flush with the body with regular sandpaper and sand the area lightly with 400-grit wet sandpaper. Prime the area where the putty was applied. In most cases, the complete body need not be primed at this time. The more paint you have to apply, the less detail there will be in any trim items painted over.

For this body, flat white paint was used as a primer because the body was white. When the primer is dry, sand the complete model with 600-grit wet sandpaper. Be careful when you are sanding over the areas where you applied putty. If you sand through the primer to the putty, prime that area again. You do not want any putty showing through the primer. When the car is completely sanded smooth, you can paint it as described in Chapter 3.

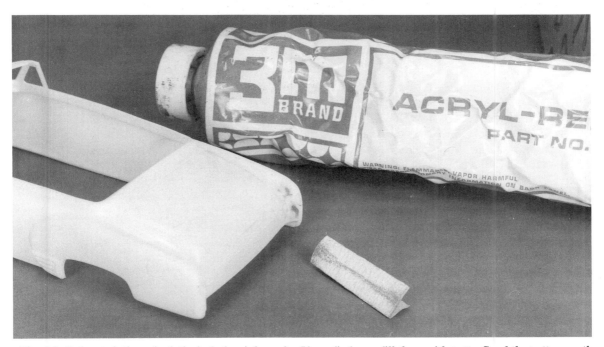

Fig. 4-9. Before painting, check the body for sink marks. If you find any, fill them with putty. Sand the putty smooth when it has dried. Then apply a coat of primer.

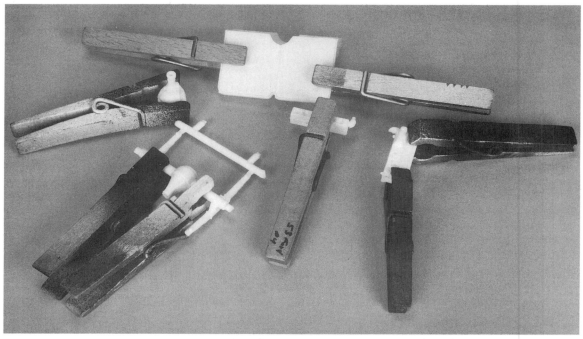

Fig. 4-10. While the painted body is drying, glue all parts of more than one piece together (seats, engine blocks, etc.). Use liquid glue, painting on an extra coat of glue on the outside seams.

DETAIL PAINTING

When it comes to painting the small parts in the kit, glue as many together that will be painted the same color as possible (Fig. 4-10). This makes painting easier and final assembly easier and quicker. When the glue is dry, file and/or sand the seams down to give the part a one-piece look; putty any gaps that are visible. Sand the seam with 400-grit wet sandpaper, and you are ready to paint the parts (Fig. 4-11).

Before painting the small parts, separate them according to the colors they will be painted. Clip the parts from the runners so a piece of the tree remains to use as a holder for painting. Trim off any flash before painting. (Flash is the thin wisps of plastic that result when two pieces of a mold don't fit together precisely.)

When the paint is dry, cut the parts from the runners and touch up the bare spots. When these are dry, they can be assembled.

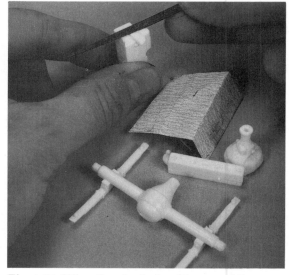

Fig. 4-11. When the glue is dry, file or sand the seams down to give the part a one-piece look. Putty any gaps that are visible. Sand the seam with 400-grit wet sandpaper.

CHARTPACK TAPE

Few modelers, if any, have a hand steady enough to paint two-tone interiors. Don't be sloppy about it, but if the dividing line between the colors isn't perfect, the parts can usually be saved with Chartpack tape in 1/64-inch widths. Chartpack makes several types of tape. For this job, use crepe tape.

Apply the tape to the edges to cover any flaws. After the tape is in place, spray on a coat of flat clear to help keep the tape in place for a long time. Chartpack tapes come in a great many colors and sizes (including a chrome Mylar tape). It is available at many art or industrial art supply stores (Figs. 4-12 and 4-13).

SEMIGLOSS FINISHES

Semigloss finishes are desirable in many applications. The easiest way to achieve a semigloss finish is to first spray the area with a flat color. When the surface is dry, apply a coat of clear gloss paint. This will give you a good semigloss finish. As an example, the chassis for the 1951 Chevy was first painted flat black, and then the gas tank was brush painted silver. When the gas tank dried, the entire unit was sprayed with gloss clear for a semigloss finish when dry. (See Fig. 4-14).

In addition, some of the floorboard was molded in with the frame (as they are on most kits). The floorboard area should be a flat color, because it

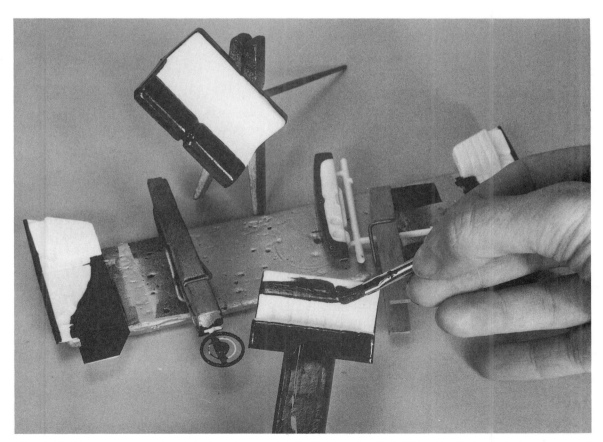

Fig. 4-12. If you want a two-tone interior, always paint the lighter color first. When the first color is dry, the second can be painted on.

Fig. 4-13. *If you are lucky enough to have the interior molded in one chosen color, paint on the second color, let it dry, then scrape off excess paint from the ridges. Once excess paint has been either scraped off or touched up, it's a good idea to cover the parting line with 1/64-inch black crepe tape.*

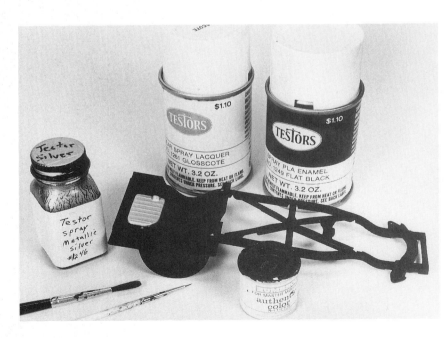

Fig. 4-14. *When painting the chassis assembly, spray flat black first if there are any floorboards molded in. Paint the frame, gas tank, or any other parts molded on the basic chassis.*

looks better and gives a better contrast to the semi-gloss black frame. To correct this, spray some clear flat paint out on a file card and brush paint the floorboard area with the clear flat. The floorboards now look like flat black again.

Getting a good semigloss out of glossy colors is a bit of a problem, because you can't just spray the clear flat over the gloss and get a semigloss; you will get a true flat. Experiment by spraying the clear flat over the gloss from a greater than normal distance. By just dusting on the clear flat, you might be able to get the semigloss, but that is not assured. In most cases, just painting on the clear flat and then buffing it with a finger after the paint is dry will give a good enough result.

CORRECTING WARPAGE

Excess heat can sometimes warp chassis (Fig. 4-15). The first step to correct the warp is to place pieces of plastic under the front and rear wheel, opposite of the wheel that is not touching in the front and under the rear wheel on the side that is not touching (Fig. 4-16). Use rubber bands to bring the raised wheel in contact with the base; base is a 1″ thick block of balsa wood.

With the chassis set up, apply heat to the frame (Fig. 4-16). Not too much or the complete assembly can be ruined. The heat from a high intensity lamp is ideal. After the chassis has been heated up a while, remove the heat and let the chassis cool. Remove the rubber bands and plastic blocks. If the chassis is still warped, do this all again, but leave the heat in place a few minutes longer. When done correctly the frame should once again be sitting level—all four wheels on the ground (Fig. 4-18).

CHROME FOIL TRIM

Before there was Bare-Metal Foil, model cars could never be considered truly complete. No matter how steady a hand a person had in painting the chrome trim, it was still just painted on silver, and it didn't look much like chrome trim. Bare-Metal Foil changed that and, properly applied, it makes a model car look complete and highly realistic.

Fig. 4-15. Warped chassis.

53

Fig. 4-16. Secure frame to wooden block with rubber bands.

Fig. 4-17. Applying heat to warped frame.

Bare-Metal Foil really isn't hard to use, but it is not a process you should rush. See Figs. 4-19 through 4-31. To adhere well, the area to which the foil is applied should be clean and free of greasy fingerprints. Have a small container of soapy water handy and wash that area. Wipe the area dry before applying the foil.

Use a Sharp Blade

If the #11 blade in your X-Acto knife is not sharp, you will end up tearing the Bare-Metal Foil rather than cutting it. This is why I have a second knife for my general hobby work. I keep a sharp blade handy just for cutting the Bare-Metal Foil. The general hobby work knife is used to cut the foil from the sheet. The instructions with the foil tell you just about all you need to know, but it should be stressed that you do not need to apply a lot of pressure to the knife to cut the foil. The more pressure you use, the harder it will be to do a good job of trimming the foil.

Both round and flat toothpicks are needed, in most cases, to get the foil in firm contact with the part being covered. To make the tool more useful, file the rounded end of the flat toothpick to a chisel point. This will allow you to really get the foil in place.

Cleaning Up

Once the excess foil is removed, an adhesive film might remain on the model. This can usually be removed by going over the area with a damp cloth. Rubbing too hard, however, could scratch the paint. Remove the residue quickly. The longer it is on, the harder it will be to remove. If you really have trouble getting it off a plastic polish or wax will usually remove the film. In 99 percent of the cases, normal rubbing with a soapy damp cloth will remove the residue.

THE LITTLE THINGS

To me, nothing ruins the look of an otherwise well-detailed model car than to see that the inside of the body was not painted. This would almost always be visible if you turned the model over, and it would

Fig. 4-18. Corrected frame.

Fig. 4-19. Now the step that adds
the finishing touch to a model car:
detailing the chrome moldings.
Many people still use chrome paint
for this, but it takes a very steady
hand, and it is still just painted silver, not chrome. With Bare-Metal
Foil, a true chrome appearance is
possible.

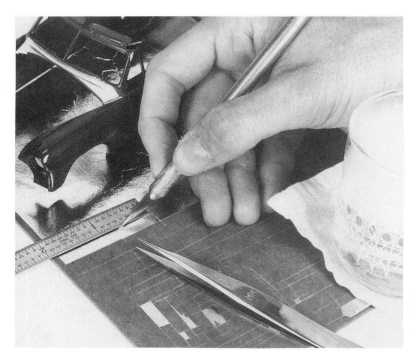

Fig. 4-20. Start by cutting a strip of foil large enough to completely cover the part to be chromed. Clean off the area of the body first by washing it with a mild detergent.

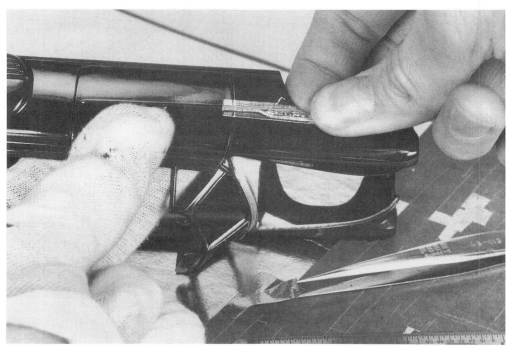

Fig. 4-21. Lift the foil from its backing and apply it to the part to be covered. Press it in firm contact with your finger or thumb.

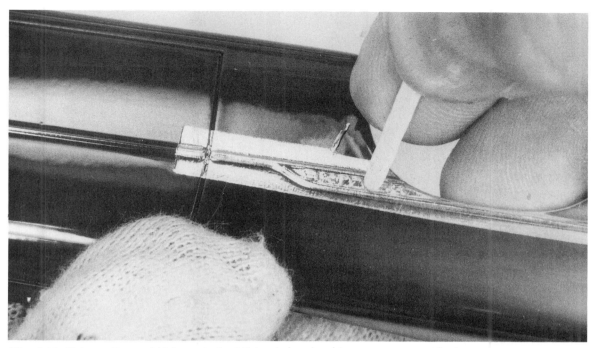

Fig. 4-22. Using a flat toothpick, work the foil in place to completely conform to the part being covered. Go over the outside edge of the part first, then keep rubbing the part with the toothpick until the foil is in complete contact with the part. All the detail should be visible through the foil. If it isn't, keep working the foil in place until it is.

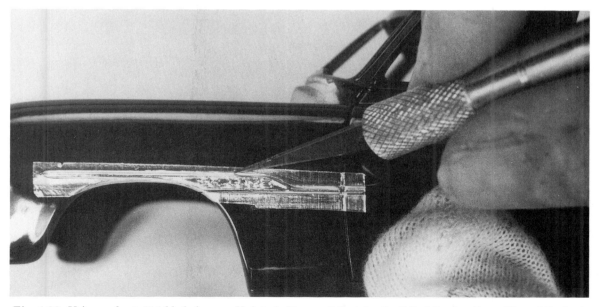

Fig. 4-23. Using a sharp #11 blade in your X-Acto knife, carefully trim the foil, following the outline of the part. After you have cut through the foil, go over the outline of the part with the flat toothpick again.

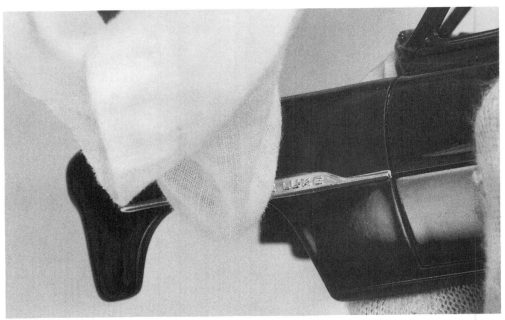

Fig. 4-24. *Remove the excess foil and burnish the foil in place with a soft cloth (which buffs the chrome to a high luster as well). If any adhesive from the foil is left on the body after you remove the excess, wash it away with the cloth.*

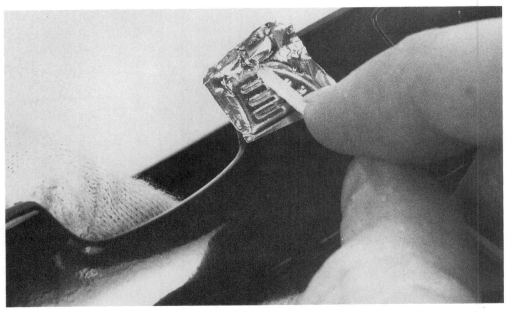

Fig. 4-25. *Compound curves are a lot of fun to cover! Carefully apply a piece large enough to cover the part. Now, slowly work the foil into contact with the part, being careful to not get wrinkles in the foil or to tear it. If the foil wrinkles badly, remove the piece and start again, being more careful.*

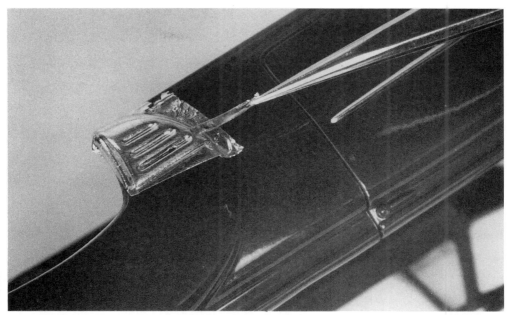

Fig. 4-26. The foil will only stretch so far. If you should come up with a tear in a deep recess, cut a narrow piece and try to work it in place. If this is not successful, you must once again start over, being even more careful.

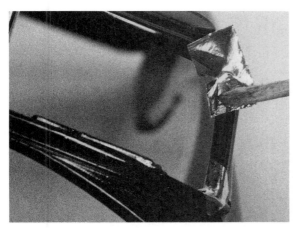

Fig. 4-27. To cover the framework of windshields, rear windows and the like, apply pieces of the foil to the corners first, covering window dividers first as shown. Corners are like compound curves, though the foil can usually be split and pressed down on the inside as this area will be painted over anyway. Some patching may be necessary. It is now a simple matter to apply strips of foil to the remaining surfaces of the framework. Trim the foil when all the strips are firmly in place.

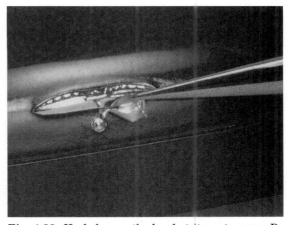

Fig. 4-28. Keyholes are the hardest items to cover. Because of their size there is not much area for the foil to get a good grip, and cutting them is hard, because they are small and round. Really take your time here. Door handles and emblems are other tricky parts, sometimes requiring two pieces of foil.

Fig. 4-29. Vent windows present about the same problem as the other framework type assemblies, although you might not have to foil the corners first. Do the edges first, then get the corners if they need it.

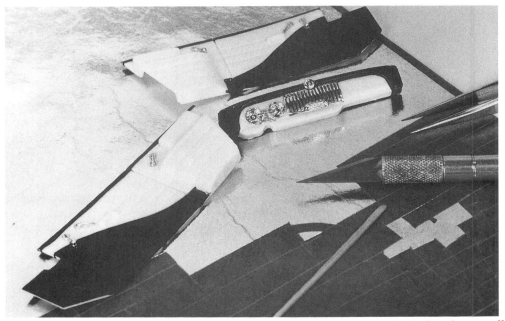

Fig. 4-30. You should apply foil to all door handles and other chrome trim items in the interior as well.

Fig. 4-31. With care and patience, there is almost nothing you can't cover in Bare-Metal Foil, even emblems like this.

certainly cost you points if the model is entered in a contest. Paint the entire inside of the model in flat black. Paint everything, because you never know what areas might be visible once the chassis is in place.

Start by painting all outside edges. Use your finger to wipe any excess paint off the edges before the paint has a chance to dry (Fig. 4-32). Do a short strip and be sure to wipe the paint off your finger with a paper towel before going on. It is the "little things" like this that can add so much to the finished model. In most cases, you hardly notice that they were ever done, but they are very noticeable if you don't do them.

TAILLIGHTS AND TURN SIGNALS

More and more kits are made with the taillights molded to the bezel units and not molded separately in clear red plastic (as was the case in the '60s). It is easy to see this from the model companies' standpoint. It costs much more to tool separate pieces

for the taillights and to separately mold them in clear red plastic.

When the taillight area is molded into the chromed bezel, you can achieve a very realistic looking taillight by simply painting it with Testor's Ruby Red #1529 (Fig. 4-33). In fact, this almost looks better than if the taillight were molded in clear red plastic.

One of the benefits of the growing popularity of the model car hobby is the many additional paints being produced for the car modeler. Besides the auto paint Testor is producing, they are also making a true amber paint, along with a paint for taillights. The taillight paint isn't as important as the amber, because Testor's old Ruby Red Metalflake was great for taillights. But it was almost impossible to mix up a decent amber paint, and thankfully, we don't have to now.

When you have to add turn signals to the side of the body, use Bare-Metal Foil to cover these side markers as you would any other chrome object. Paint in the markers as you normally would with red

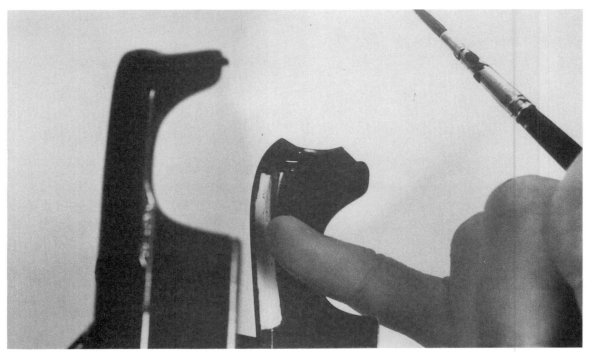

Fig. 4-32. Wipe excess paint off the edges before the paint dries.

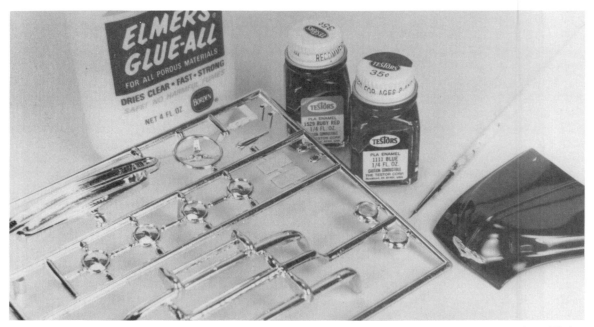

Fig. 4-33. Glue clear headlight lens in place with white glue. Depending on the model, either glue the taillights in place, or in this case, paint them in. Also paint any emblem parts now.

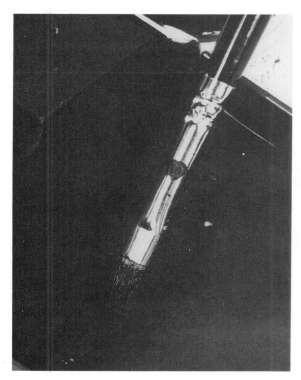

taillights and amber for the turn signals. The Bare-Metal Foil not only serves to cover the chrome bezel, but is also a chrome base for the red and amber colored paints.

For additional finish details, refer to Figs. 4-34 and 4-35. The completed model is shown in Fig. 4-36.

REPLICA STOCK MODELS

Building showroom replica stock models can be very satisfying. They are among the most difficult models to build, however, because gathering the information to make them accurate can be difficult. If you can find an actual example of the car of which you will be making the model, you should have little trouble in producing an accurate model. Not many model builders are fortunate enough to be able to locate a real car and must rely on other sources for the information.

Restoration Guides

Enthusiast magazines that cover the car of which you are making a replica can be a good source of infor-

Fig. 4-34. (above) After you epoxy the interior in place (and any other items like front fender wells, etc.), paint over the epoxy with flat black to hide it from view. Make sure the inside of the body is completely painted in flat black; nothing ruins the looks of a model more than having an unpainted section showing through when you turn the model over to inspect the chassis.

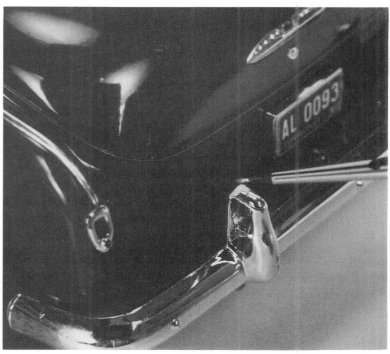

Fig. 4-35. (left) The final step is to touch up all visible glue spots, chips in the paint, and all pieces of chrome where they were cut from the tree.

63

Fig. 4-36. (above) The finished model straight out of the box. Nothing added but paint, foil, and your time.

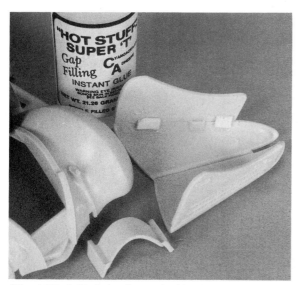

Fig. 4-37. (left) A few braces inside the hood will make this assembly stronger. Do this while the body is still taped to the fenders, using them as a guide to get these parts lined up correctly.

mation, but even the best of the magazines from the time the car was new, or any of the excellent old car magazines today, will likely not give you all the information needed. Original or reproduction sales brochures are also a help, and are recommended.

Actual restoration guides are your best friend here, however, and while not many guides are available as this is written, more will likely be published as the old car hobby becomes more and more popular. For the Ertl/AMT 1936 Fords, the best book you could buy is *The Early Ford V8 as Henry Built It*, by Edward P. Francis and George DeAngelis. This book covers all Ford body styles from 1932 to 1938. Body colors are mentioned, even the short run special colors; interior colors are covered well; and there are so many detail photographs of all types that if you are building any model cars from this era, consider this book a must-purchase. Books that concern themselves with the car you are interested in modeling are worth searching out, and the latest Classic Motorbook catalog is the best place to look for in-print books.

Hood Modifications

The final fit of the hood on the 1936 Ford is not the best (Figs. 4-37 and 4-38), especially the left-hand (driver's) side. With the hood side panel glued to the top of the hood, there is a very minor gap (Fig. 4-39). It would look best if this gap were filled. To fill this gap, cut a narrow strip of sheet styrene plastic and glue it to the back of the left hood side. When the glue is totally dry, first sand the plastic strip to

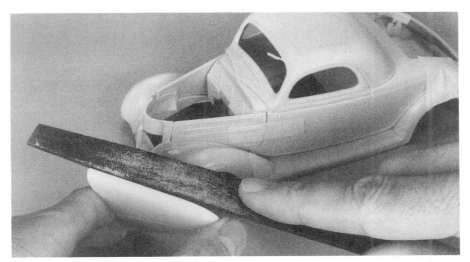

Fig. 4-38. The fit of the hood is important, and it will take a bit of corrective work to get it to fit better. First tape the body to the fenders, then tape the hood side panels to this, then tape the grille shell in place. A little filing and filling here will result in a better fit on the final model.

Fig. 4-39. The gap between the back of the hood side panel and the body really should be filled before the model is painted. Refer to the text for details.

the thickness of the hood side. You can now sand this small extension down to match the contour of the body, eliminating the excess gap between the back of the hood and the body. Putty any gaps to fully smooth this extension piece to the hood side, then just paint as usual. This method can be used to fill any gap that is too large to look natural on a model car (Fig. 4-40).

Engine Wiring

The 1936 Ford is also a fairly simple engine to which to add basic wiring. There are many firms selling wire for scale engines, and all of them look pretty good. For a first project, though, you can get by with a few household or craft items. For this engine, I used thread for the ignition wires, and some very old #24 copper wire for fuel lines (Fig. 4-41). Run the thread through wax to remove the fuzzy appearance and give it some body. When attaching the thread/wire to the tube (loom), you can use either epoxy or one of the gap-filling superglues (Fig. 4-42). I also drilled holes in the distributor, on the front of the engine block, for the loom (a 1/16-inch piece of plastic rod). This allows a stronger bond for the loom. When the thread has been glued in place, paint the connectors flat black; actually, it is best to paint

the entire thread, from the spark plug to the loom (Fig. 4-43).

Strengthen Windshield Frame

If you are building the roadster version of this car, it is suggested you make some modifications to the chrome windshield frame. As it comes from the kit, the windshield is supposed to be just glued to the cowl, a butt joint. This type of joint has two disadvantages. First, it is a very weak joint. Second, it is very hard to glue/epoxy the frame in place without getting glue marks on the model. By adding pins to the bottom of the windshield frame, and then drilling holes in the cowl to accept them, you end up with a strong joint, and less of a chance of getting glue on the cowl (Fig. 4-44). It is also really quite easy to do and takes little time. When drilling the holes in the cowl, and when gluing the windshield frame in place, use the up top to position the windshield frame. Further detailing is shown in Figs. 4-45 through 4-48.

Chassis

Detailing the chassis can include adding the brake lines, but if you are not ready for that, you might

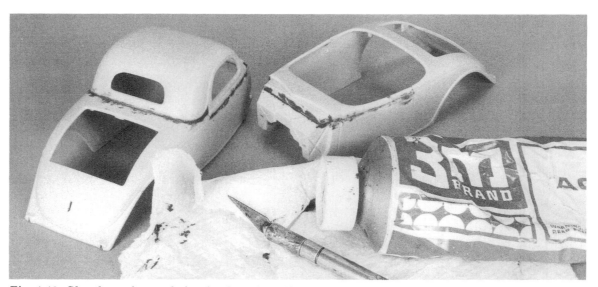

Fig. 4-40. Glue the roof or cowl piece in place (depending on which version you are building). When the glue is dry, putty any gaps between these pieces to make the body look like a one-piece assembly.

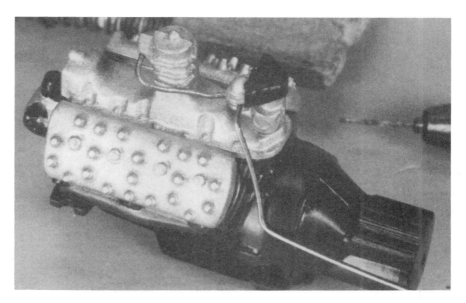

Fig. 4-41. The engine for the 1936 Ford is fairly easy to add simple wiring to, making it a good starting project. Drill holes in the carb and fuel pump for fuel lines; paint these pieces and, when dry, glue them in place on the painted engine. Run a fuel line (#24 copper wire) between the holes; a second line runs from fuel pump to gas tank (install after engine has been glued to the frame).

Fig. 4-42. The ignition wires for this Ford flathead run to a tube, which then goes to the distributor. Bend this tube from ¹/₁₆-inch plastic rod. Before epoxying this rod to the engine, drill holes for the wires. Paint the rod black and attach the wires when the paint dries; glue the rod in place. Cut the wire to size and glue these to the sparkplugs.

Fig. 4-43. AMT didn't include the voltage regulator, but it is easily made from a piece of the body-colored side pipes; just a short cylinder on top of the generator, painted silver. Drill a hole through the regulator and run a wire through it. Bend each end of the wire down, drill two holes in the top of the generator for these wires, and epoxy unit in place.

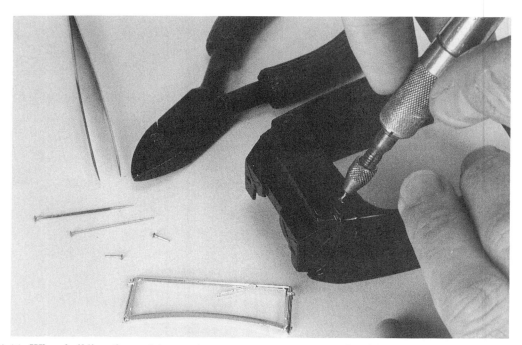

Fig. 4-44. When building the roadster version, you can get a stronger windshield frame by drilling small holes in the bottom of the windshield frame. Epoxy cut-off straight pins in these holes, then drill holes in the cowl to accept the pins. When epoxying the windshield frame in place on the finished model, use the top to get the angle correct.

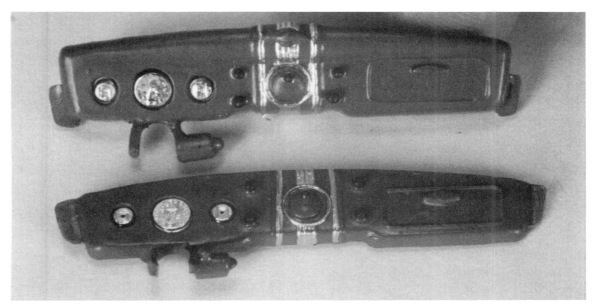

Fig. 4-45. *Once the instrument panels are painted and dry, Bare-Metal Foil makes detailing the chrome trim easy.*

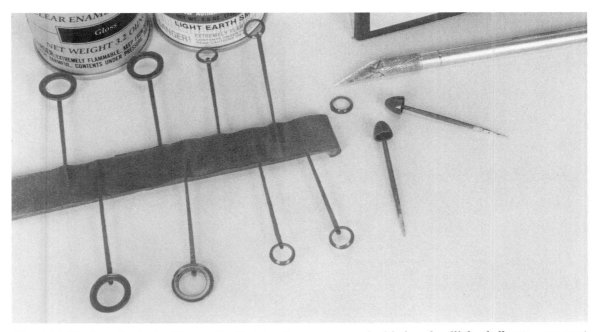

Fig. 4-46. *To clean the flash off parts like the trim rings and rear wheel halves, headlight shells, etc., you must remove them from the trees. To make painting these small parts easier after being removed from the trees, attach these parts to flat toothpicks with epoxy. When the paint is dry, remove the toothpick and remove any epoxy/wood from the back of the part.*

Fig. 4-47. A couple of braces make attaching the body to the fender assembly much easier. Braces for the back of the body were made from thin sheet brass, bent to fit, then epoxied in place. Make sure these braces don't interfere with the frame. Touch up before epoxying the frame in place.

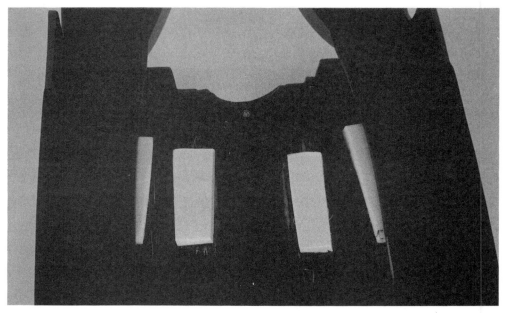

Fig. 4-48. Strips of scrap plastic can be glued to the interior to allow you to glue directly to the chassis. Use thin pieces and build them up until they nearly touch the chassis. This will make it much easier to epoxy the chassis to the body, allowing for a stronger bond with no chance of having any epoxy joints visible.

Fig. 4-49. The completed model.

want to just dress up the chassis with a little paint. First, paint the chassis assembly flat black. Follow this with a coat of Testor's Glosscote. This will give the chassis a semigloss look. Next, paint the floor in a wood color, taking care to not get paint on the frame rails. Leave the frame rails and battery box black. The exhaust system is painted in a steel color. Axles are also given the semigloss black treatment. The gas tank can be painted a steel or aluminum color. This detail painting doesn't take a lot of time, but it will add a lot to the looks of the model should anyone pick it up and turn it over; which is what most people seem to do!

By using the material available today, you should be able to come up with a showroom stock model that looks correct. Just remember, no one source available (as this is written) has all the information you will need. By gathering all the material that you can on the real car the results will look good and much of the enjoyment of building the model will be in the research you have done. Learn all you can about your subject (Fig. 4-49).

Chapter 5
Metal Models

Die-cast metal models are becoming more popular today. Unfortunately, few of these models are being produced as kits. Hubley was one of the first to produce a good quality die-cast kit, and their Ford Model A series came in many body styles, with other marques soon joining this series. The Hubley tools were sold to Gabriel, who produced the series for many years and added some excellent Ford Ts to the line. Unfortunately, soon after the first release of this book came out, all the Gabriel kits were dropped from the line. These die-cast kit tools were eventually sold to Scale Models, who released some of the Ford As and the Chevys in 1987 and 1988. Other kits will follow, including the Duesenberg used to illustrate this feature. The tips are the same for any of these kits, though—just the models change.

For a while, Monogram Models was in the die-cast kit business with a series of excellent $\frac{1}{24}$-scale kits. These kits differed from the Hubley/Gabriel models in that only the body and its related parts were in die-cast metal, with all the other parts in plastic. The series didn't survive long, though, and some of the tooling was converted to produce plastic bodies to go with the rest of the plastic parts. As this is written, Burago still produces kits of many of their die-cast models in $\frac{1}{24}$ and $\frac{1}{18}$ scale. Unlike the Gabriel/Hubley kits, the Burago models come with flash-free prepainted bodies, making basic assembly extremely easy. There are also some very expensive die-cast based kits, so there *is* a choice in die-cast kits—not a big one, but a choice still.

METAL FLASH

When you first open a Gabriel/Hubley kit (and very likely the Scale Models reissues), you are in for a bit of a shock. To say the least, the flash attached to the metal parts looks to be almost an impossible obstacle to building the kit! It looks worse than it really is. Most of the flash can be removed with a pair of standard pliers (see Fig. 5-1). Once the flash is removed, the mold lines and edges can be filed down (followed with sanding) and treated like any other kit from there on.

JOINING THE BODY PIECES

Most of the old Hubley kits came with two-piece (or more in some cases) bodies. With the Duesenberg, the body sections are almost completely covered by one accessory or another. But still, the body should be molded to resemble a one-piece unit. Once the body pieces have been epoxied together, apply strips of epoxy-soaked cloth to the inside seams. This step is similar to using glue and cloth on a plastic model. Do not, however, apply the cloth to the underside of the cowl where it could interfere with the location of the instrument panel.

The large screw that holds the body pieces together should also be filed down flush with the body and then puttied smooth (Figs. 5-2 through 5-6).

PRIME THE BODY

Almost without exception, all die-cast metal bodies have little "imperfections" in them known as *rills*. "Imperfections" is not the correct word, because rills are common to all die-cast metal models; it is common to the casting method. Rills are small crack-like fissures in the surface of the metal. If they are not filled in and smoothed over, they will ruin the looks of the finished model.

If the surface flaws are large enough to be visible, putty them before you paint the first coat of primer. You can easily see the small rills if you lightly sand the body. The rills will stand out as dark irregular lines against the shiny metal body. Once all the larger rills (and any other visible flaws) are put-

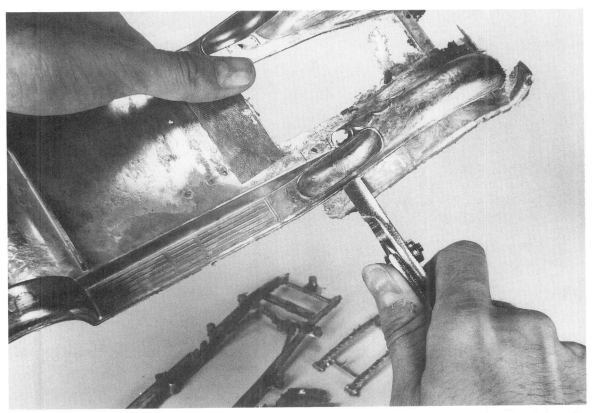

Fig. 5-1. With almost any die-cast metal kit, your first job will be to remove the flash. When the flash is really bad, remove it with pliers. File and sand all flash and any mold marks from all the metal parts. The more files you have, the easier it will be.

Fig. 5-2. Before doing any finishing, check the metal parts for fit. In models like this, it is possible to almost complete the model in the unfinished stage: good to check the parts for fit. Tap the screw holes.

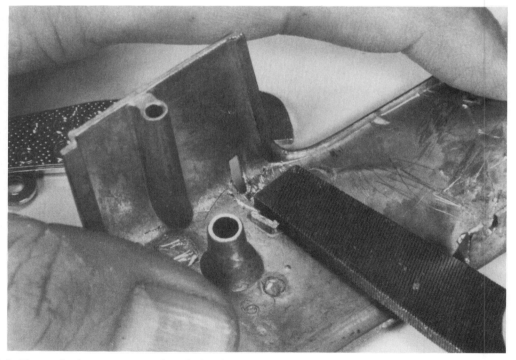

Fig. 5-3. To get the instrument panel to fit in place once the body is molded together, file one of the mounting tabs off. The other side can be left alone.

Fig. 5-4. Work quickly after you have mixed a large batch of epoxy. Apply some epoxy to the two body halves where they join. Use the screw to secure the two body pieces and set the body on the fenders. To add strength to the body, epoxy pieces of cloth over the seams.

Fig. 5-5. File down the body seams so both sides line up. Also file down any mounting screws used to hold the body together. Putty all gaps and screw mounting holes.

Fig. 5-6. On dual-cowl phaeton bodies, the second cowl could present a problem when the two body halves are joined. If you file one of the mounting lugs on the cowl down, you will usually be able to spread the body enough to get the cowl in place. Don't file the lug so much the cowl falls out; check while filing.

tied over and sanded smooth, spray on a coat of a metal primer. Tempo #7-4000 works very well. Sand the primer down after it is dry. You might need to sand and prime several times until the primed surface is free of visible rills and other defects.

With the metal pieces primed, spray on the automotive paints with no fear of crazing. That feeling alone makes working with metal body parts very attractive.

Once the body is painted (two-tone in this case), you can rub out the paint. Rubbing out a classic or any other older car is a lot harder than rubbing out a modern car. On the classics there are many projections in the way that make rubbing out these bodies less than fun. If you do rub through, however, touch-up is fairly easy.

WHITEWALL TIRES

Because the tires in Gabriel kits are made from rubberlike compound, the normal method of applying whitewalls doesn't apply (see Chapter 6). The paper transfers for whitewalls don't work very well because the side wall of the tires are on too much of an angle, and the paper tends to wrinkle no matter how careful you are.

In this case, true whitewall tire paint works the best. How to set up the wheels for painting the whitewall is described in Figs. 5-7 and 5-8. When applying the paint, do so in heavy coats. Work the paint to the outer edge of the whitewall. Take care not to go beyond the whitewall area. If you do, wipe the excess off before it has had a chance to dry. The paint is not brushed on. Dip the brush in the paint and don't wipe any off. Instead of brushing the paint in place, just dab it in place.

Done properly, with the body rubbed to within an inch of its life, the completed model is a masterpiece. The manufacturer has done a good job with

Fig. 5-7. For whitewalls on this Gabriel Duesenberg, first install the rear wheel part. Apply whitewall tire paint thickly; dab it in place rather than brush. Allow plenty of drying time.

Fig. 5-8. To get the wheelfront in place on the tire, trim the rim down so it is flush with the wheel sides. This way, the outer wheel part can be glued in place without harm to the whitewall.

Fig. 5-9. When correctly painted and rubbed out, the look of the completed model is something very special.

these kits, but it is up to you to bring them to life (Fig. 5-9).

REWORKING
FACTORY-ASSEMBLED MODELS

With the advent of the factory-assembled die-cast model in the larger ½₅ or ¼₄ scale (most of the older die-cast models were made to the "collectors scale" of ¼₃), a new field opened up for the general model car builder. Many of the larger scale die-cast models are very well detailed, but in many cases, the engine detail leaves much to be desired. Sometimes, the colors the factory painted the models in were not always the greatest, and sometimes the paint jobs were even worse. After all, these are mass produced items, and a few poorly painted ones will show up in the best of lines. And at times, the casting themselves had flaws that were not hidden by the paint jobs.

Because general detailing on these models is usually as good as any kit, the currently available models can be considered possible fodder for the model car builder. And because most of these larger models are assembled with screws, they can usually be disassembled completely if you are careful. There can be a problem with older models. Once you

Fig. 5-10. The first step in refinishing a factory assembled die-cast model car is to remove any self-stick decals. Be careful in removing these if you wish to use them on the refinished model.

repaint a factory assembled die-cast model, its value to a collector drops greatly. That is no problem if you never intend to sell the piece, but you can never be entirely sure of that. I suggest that you stick to repainting one of the great many currently available models.

Once you have the model disassembled, it is a simple procedure to strip the paint from the metal parts. See Figs. 5-10 through 5-12. Products such as Zip Strip remove the unwanted paint in no time. Follow the procedure on the can of stripper you are using. To apply Zip Strip, a wide flat brush is best. Allow the Zip Strip to work on the paint, then rinse it off under running water. An old toothbrush is helpful for removing stubborn spots of paint. Work on only a small area at a time. Once you have stripped the paint off the model, treat it like you would any other die-cast metal model car kit.

WHITE-METAL KITS

In the late 1970s, a new metal kit came on strong. These kits were produced to ¼₃ scale in a material called *white metal*. This is a soft metal, and though it is metal, it is almost as easy to work in as plastic. The white-metal manufacturers are mainly located

Fig. 5-11. Now completely disassemble the model, taking care not to break anything. Many plastic parts are heat-sealed in place. Cut through the tabs with an X-Acto knife and remove the part. Nothing should be left on the body.

Fig. 5-12. Some models come riveted together. In these cases, you must drill through the rivet to allow disassembly of the model; epoxy chassis in place when you assemble the model again.

in England, France, Germany, and Italy. Although there are few white-metal kit producers in the United States, there are several who make assembled models, and if you count HO-scale producers, there are a fair number of American white-metal models being produced.

White-metal kits have gained great popularity for one main reason. The manufacturers make models of cars that would never be attempted by the major kit manufacturers. This is mainly because the cars being modeled would not be popular enough for a mass market.

White-metal molds do not cost as much to produce as a die-cast injection tool. Unfortunately, a mold for a white-metal model can only produce about 1000 models before it is worn out. Then the model either goes out of production or another set of molds is made. White-metal kits tend to be on the expensive side because so much hand work goes into them. Another factor is the limited production.

Early white-metal kits didn't find much acceptance in the United States mainly because most Americans who like 1/43-scale models are not kit builders. Also, many of these early white-metal models were on the crude side. Competition between the various manufacturers helped change that, with each trying to add a bit more detail than the other. The builder has been the beneficiary of this competition, and some white-metal kits rival the die-cast model for detail.

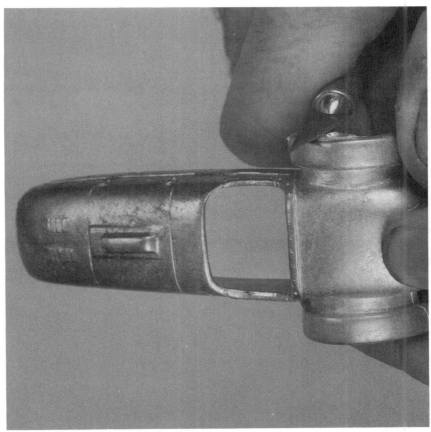

Fig. 5-13. As with any metal kit, first trim all flash from the parts. With a white metal kit, the flash can be removed with a knife, though some may need to be filed.

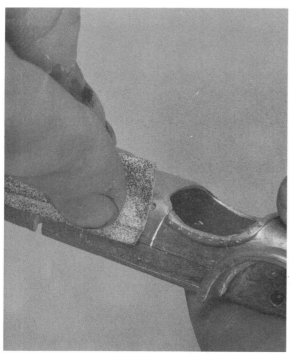

Some of the top white-metal companies will probably not continue to make better detailed models. They have pretty much reached the stage where they really don't need any added detailing. Before long, I am sure most of the other white-metal producers will be bringing up their standards to equal the best.

Uncommon Cars

If you like not-so-common cars or if you are a racing car buff, white-metal kits are something you should check out. The worst thing about most white-metal models is that they are very easy to build. This creates a problem. Because the average white-metal kit can be built quickly, you could spend a fortune keeping yourself in these models. Although I know the kit producers wouldn't mind, other people in your family might. Imagine that, will you!

Soft Metal

Like any regular kit, white-metal model kits are available in varying degrees of difficulty. The Kurtis 500 Roadster in 1/43 scale in the Americana series by Mikansue of England is a very simple kit. There aren't many parts and no major building prob-

Fig. 5-14. Next, remove all mold parting lines. Again, because the metal is softer, regular sandpaper should do the job.

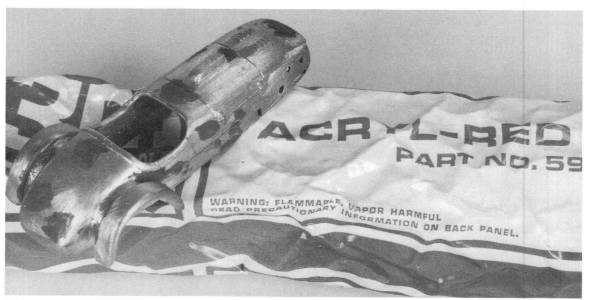

Fig. 5-15. Before priming, fill in any visible sink marks, rills, or other imperfections on the body.

lems. If you are just getting into white-metal kits, start out with a simple easy-to-assemble kit. If you don't know anyone who has first-hand building experience with a white-metal kit, ask a dealer about the best kits. They can give you some examples that will surely hook you on these model cars.

One of the nicest things about white-metal kits is the ease of working with the soft metal. It is al-

Fig. 5-16. It is also a good idea to scribe the body lines a little deeper. Again, because of the soft metal, the lines are not hard to deepen.

Fig. 5-17. The final step before priming is to drill out any flashed over holes. Check the parts to make sure they will fit in the holes.

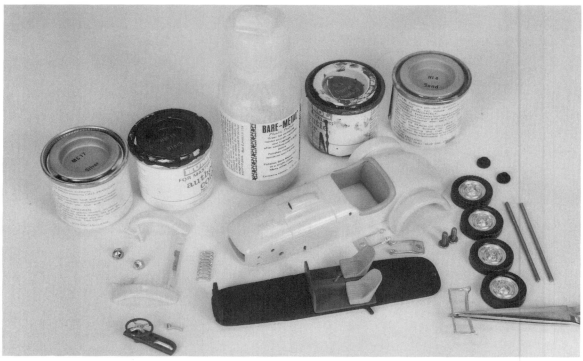

Fig. 5-18. Rub the body out if you used automotive paints, paint all remaining accessories, and apply any decals that may be in the kit. Epoxy any clear parts in place and then finish assembling the model.

most easier than working with plastic. Because the bodies are of metal, any type of paint can be used on them. Although I am not ready to sell my collection of rare old unbuilt plastic kits, I am very excited about white-metal model cars.

Even though the development of the white-metal kit (and it needs to be mentioned that more companies are producing factory finished white-metal models, mainly because there are more collectors into 1/43-scale than there are builders) is fairly new, there is a newer medium still, and this seems to have even more promise. The 1/43-scale resin-cast kits are true jewels, generally having even more detail than the white-metal kits. The advantages of the white-metal kits are also a feature of the resin kits—ease of building because of their simplicity, small runs of unusual prototypes, compatibility with any paint, etc. Resin models also come in factory-built form from many manufacturers. White metal or resin, if you like 1/43-scale cars, the variety offered here is amaz-

Fig. 5-19. The finished model is quite an attractive piece, especially when you consider how little time was spent in getting the model to this stage.

ing, from little known European makes to true Classics to NASCAR racers, there is something for every automotive miniature collector's taste.

For construction details, refer to Figs. 5-13 through 5-18. The finished model is shown in Fig. 5-19.

Chapter 6

Miscellaneous Tips

There is a great problem in writing down general tips when you have been building model cars for many years. The tips that might be of great help to the novice are common procedures for experts. They are taken for granted and accomplished as if they were automatic. Doing them is easy, thinking of them is difficult. With that in mind, the general tips mentioned in this chapter can be used throughout the book to detail the models. Most of the tips here apply to all the models.

FLAT BLACK WASH

Nothing makes a model car look more like a model than having a fully chromed grille. The spaces between the grille bars are meant to be black areas. The easiest way to accomplish this on the model grille is to paint it with a flat black wash (Fig. 6-1). Prepare the wash by thinning flat black to the consistency of water. The wash should be thin enough so that when you touch the tip of the paintbrush (a small pointed brush is best) to the grille, the paint flows from the brush to the area of the grille you want blanked out.

Because the wash is very thin, it will usually not stick to the raised chrome ribs. Instead, it will settle in the low areas you want flat black. If the spaces between the grille moldings are deep, it will take more paint, because the areas must be almost entirely filled with paint.

There is a problem with grilles with wide gaps between the ribs. These usually can't be filled with the thin wash. The wash just tends to crowd around the raised areas, leaving the center of the recessed area open and the chrome showing through. If you try to fill up the space with the thinned wash, you will find that instead of the paint filling in the open areas, it will run over the ribs, and the centers will still be showing chrome. The correction for this problem is shown in Fig. 6-2. Basically, it is painting the open areas with straight flat black.

When you clean the chrome as shown in Fig. 6-3, be careful that you don't rub too hard and rub the chrome off the ribs.

Besides the grilles, this type of wash is useful for many other applications in colors other than flat black. It is especially effective for dashboard detailing if the dials are chromed or covered in Bare-Metal Foil.

WHITEWALLS AND TIRE LETTERING

For most tires, gesso will work well for painting the lettering on the tires. Floquil's Polly S will also work well, however, Polly S does become brittle as it dries and can easily chip off.

The problem is finding a paint that will dry, but not be so brittle that it will chip easily. Gesso will take at least a little flexing of the tire and for this reason it is preferred. Gesso is used to prime canvas and should be carried by any art supply store. (See Figs. 6-4 through 6-5.)

If you happen to get any gesso on the ridge of the tire when painting wide whitewalls, just let it dry.

Scrape the excess off. Work carefully or you might scratch the whitewall. By scraping off any excess gesso, you should have a perfect wide whitewall.

Try to get the whitewall painted in one coat. When that isn't possible, thin a bit of the gesso (with water) in another jar and paint on one or two (or more if necessary) thin coats. Allow plenty of drying time between coats. No matter what you are using to paint a whitewall, if more than one coat is needed, the second coat should be applied with thinned paint.

ADDING SPOILERS

This tip on molding spoilers to the body—so that they will look like they are separate pieces—works well on many other applications. This technique

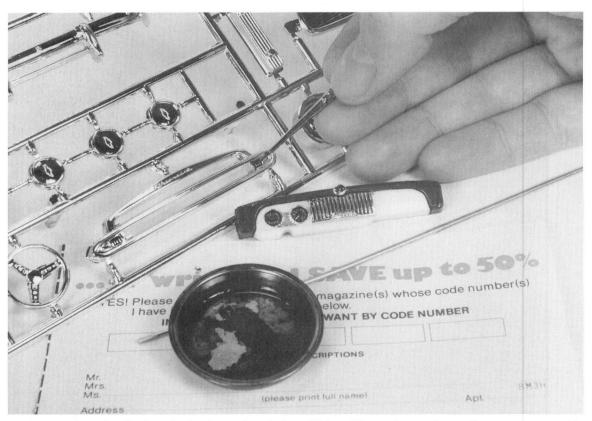

Fig. 6-1. Make a flat black wash of paint and apply it to fill in grille openings and any other areas you want to appear vacant, or highlighted.

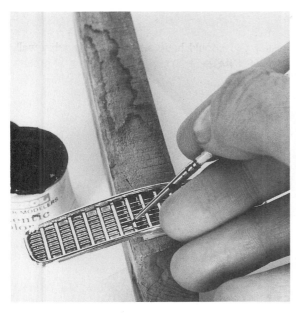

Fig. 6-2. Although the flat black wash will work for most applications, when the space between grille bars is large, it may not work too well. For these applications, apply the wash first and let it dry. When dry, if any areas of chrome are showing through, paint on flat black right out of the jar or tin to fill in the open areas.

Fig. 6-4. The only "secret" in painting the lettering on tires is to use a very fine pointed brush (00000 size). After the brush is loaded with paint roll the tip of the brush to a perfect point. You need not point the brush each time you get paint and the brush could be cleaned if it seems to be loading up on paint.

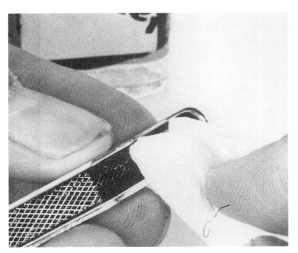

Fig. 6-3. If too much of the wash sticks to the raised area of the grille, wrap a tissue around a stiff object (like a metal ruler), and apply a drop of thinner to the tissue. Wipe the excess paint off the exposed ribs as shown.

works especially well on kits with separately molded pieces for the nose and rear deck. Just glue or epoxy these separate pieces to the body and fill in the gaps like you did for the spoiler. If the pieces are meant to look like separate pieces, the epoxy will perfectly simulate the look. When done properly, you can hardly tell the pieces you molded from the natural seams on the kit (Figs. 6-7 through 6-9).

Fig. 6-5. *There are many ways to put a wide whitewall on a tire. For most vinyl-type tires, gesso applied in heavy coats works very well. Hard, nonvinyl tires can usually be painted with Humbrol flat paints. Apply these as thickly as you would gesso. As with all whitewall tires, avoid a second coat of paint if possible. Real whitewall tire paint works well on rubber like tires.*

Fig. 6-6. *Want a narrow wall tire? Use an X-Acto Compas and white contact paper. Once you have the outside measurement for the whitewalls, cut all needed at this setting before adjusting to cut the whitewall to size. Wide walls are possible with this method as well, but make sure the contact paper does not extend into the wheel area.*

fore applying the epoxy filler. Use the "V" file for
this.

On some cars, once you glue the body pieces in place, you might have to deepen the groove be- this. The advantage of filling body seams like this is that you get a body that looks like it is one piece, but not with the seams all molded smooth.

HINGES

There are many ways to make hinges for the doors, trunk, hood, or anything else you might want to open and close (Figs. 6-10 through 6-18). The paper clip hinge is the easiest concealed hinge to make. Wire hinges are also easy to make and work well on all

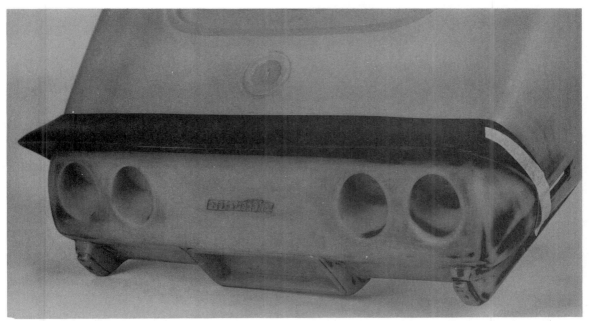

Fig. 6-7. Spoilers are a very popular item on many cars today. To give them a custom fit, first epoxy them to the body.

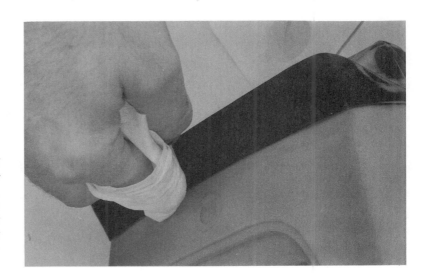

Fig. 6-8. Mix a batch of epoxy and apply it to the seam where spoiler meets body. Before the epoxy sets, wipe off all excess epoxy. This should give you a very smooth joint between body and spoiler, almost like it was molded to the body— without the one-piece look.

Fig. 6-9. *The final results after painting are very impressive, giving the impression you really worked to get the seam just right—but it is really easy to do.*

older cars with exposed hinges. Attaching wire hinges is fairly easy too, but you must remember one critical point. On older cars, with a slight curve to the body, make sure the pivot points line up for the top and bottom hinges. An example of this type of car would be the Ford Model A Sedan.

Picture it like this. The top part of the body is wider, with the body tapering in several inches toward the bottom, where the body meets the fender unit. The top hinge should be just sticking beyond the surface of the body. The pivot on the bottom hinge, on the other hand, would be several scale inches out from the body. With cars like this, you must line the pivot points up, otherwise the doors will not open correctly. Think of the pivot point running in a line perpendicular to the ground from the top hinge to the bottom hinge. The pivot point on

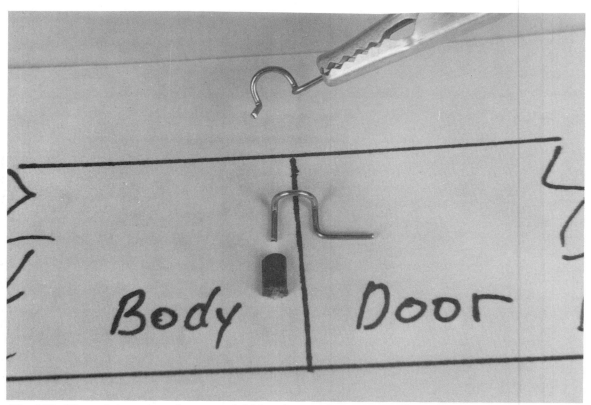

Fig. 6-10. *The easiest way to make a concealed hinge is to cut down a paper clip and bend as shown. File a notch in a piece of scrap plastic to serve as the pivot for the straight part of the hinge.*

Fig. 6-11. Glue the pivot to the body, trapping the straight part of the hinge in the notch. Allow to dry. Then either epoxy or heat sink the other end of the hinge into the door. With everything in place, you can usually remove the door from the body if necessary.

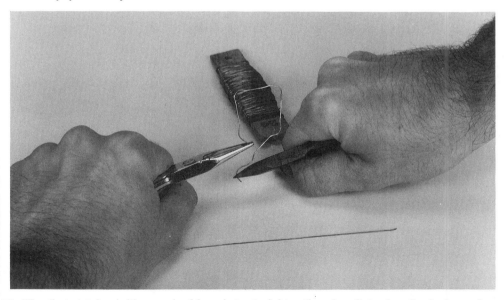

Fig. 6-12. The first step in making a wire hinge is to straighten the wire. Cut a length of wire and grasp each end with a pair of pliers. Pull taut. You might need to make several "snaps" to get all the kinks out. If you pull hard enough to break one end of the wire, it is usually as straight as you will get it.

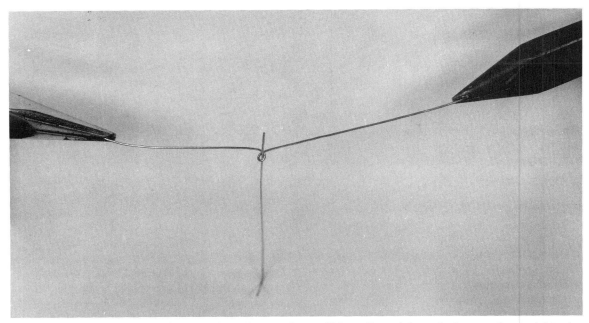

Fig. 6-13. Loop one piece of wire around another, as shown. Using pliers, tighten the loop on the straight wire. Don't pull the looped wire so tight it distorts the straight wire.

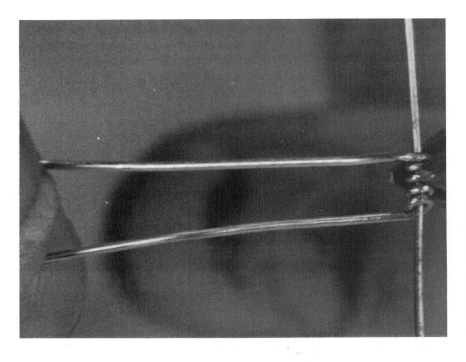

Fig. 6-14. Wrap the wire several times around the straight wire, as tightly as possible without distorting it. After several turns, bring the ends of the wire together as shown. Adjust the hinge to get a tight fit on the straight piece and straighten everything up.

the wire hinge would be what started out as the straight wire around which the other wire was wrapped several times. When you wrap the wire around the straight wire, wrap it as tightly as possible. If you don't, the finished hinge will be sloppy.

MARKING PAINT JARS

I keep all my jars and tins of paint in old model kit boxes. If you have the space, you could make narrow shelves to hold all the jars so that you could see all the labels. If space is a problem, and you must keep the jars and tins in boxes, paint the tops of the paint containers the color that is in them. This way, you will know what color is where in an instant.

CLEANING FILES

Files should be kept clean, or material will tend to build up in the ridges and cut down the efficiency of the file. The easiest way to clean the files is to brush them with a suede shoe brush. The fine wire bristles of the brush easily remove most of the excess material. When the brush does not clean out the file, however, you might have to clean out each ridge with the tip of a #11 X-Acto blade.

TAILLIGHT DETAILS

On the models that come with their taillights molded in clear red plastic, paint the back of the lens with silver paint. This will allow you to epoxy them in place with greater ease. This tip is mainly for taillights that are not glued to a dished reflector. If the taillight is glued to a reflector (similar to an old car headlight), the lens can be glued in place without painting the back of the lens. Painting the lens is mainly for the times you have to glue the taillight against a flat surface.

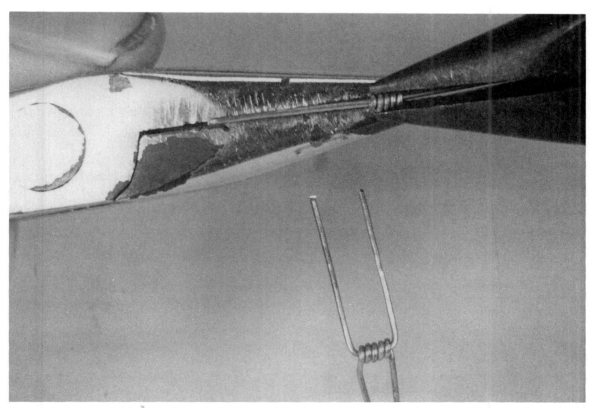

Fig. 6-15. Squeeze the looped wire around the straight wire and adjust so the wires are straight, as shown by the two pliers. Now bend the straight wire to 90-degree angles as shown on bottom hinge.

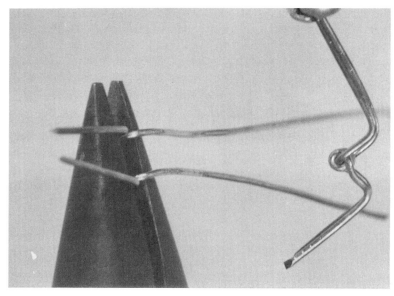

Fig. 6-16. To complete the hinges, bend the ends to 90-degree angles in opposite directions. These bends should be far enough down the wire so they are at least equal to the thickness of the plastic pieces you are hinging.

makes the kits a lot harder to build—especially for the novice.

One of the crucial areas is the side mirrors. In the '60s, these mirrors almost always had positive mounting lugs molded to them. The corresponding hole in the body was usually flashed over so that you wouldn't have to add the mirrors if you didn't want to; the choice was up to you.

On most mirrors in today's kits you are expected to just glue the mirror to the body. When there are no positive mounting locators on the mirror, this is almost impossible to do, especially if the body is painted. No matter how hard you try, if you do get the mirror glued in place without ruining the paint job, the joint will always be a weak one. Personally, I cannot understand why the companies leave something so simple, but so important, as the mounting lugs off items like mirrors. It would be no problem for them to add these mounting lugs to the part.

Because the companies are not adding these lugs to items like outside mirrors, you should (Fig. 6-19). The time you spend adding the lugs to the mirror will be more than made up during final assembly, and the frustration factor will be lessened as well. Unfortunately, it is not possible to add lugs to all mirrors.

Fig. 6-17. To attach the wire hinges, notch the door and body slightly to compensate for the thickness of the hinge. Epoxy or heat sink the hinges to the body and door.

POSITIVE MOUNTING LUGS

In today's kits, the trend is away from positive mounting lugs for almost all parts. These positive position locators are not needed for all types of parts, but some important parts lose their lugs and this

92

In those cases where you have to just glue (epoxy) the mirror to the body, you might find it easier to have the body held so that the mirror is almost balanced on the body. Apply the epoxy to the mirror mount and let it set until it is almost ready to set up. Then quickly install it on the body. Hold it in place until the epoxy has fully set up.

By tilting the body and letting the epoxy set a while, you might not even have to hold the mirror until the epoxy sets. Do only one side at a time and let the car set overnight before continuing work on it. This will assure a good strong bond between mirror mount and body. When affixing mirrors like this, they should be among the last steps in finishing the model.

SEMIGLOSS COLORS FROM JAR PAINTS

Making a semigloss jar paint is possible and desirable for a variety of applications. Before you start,

make sure that the "flat" really is a flat color and not already a semigloss color. The reason I mention this is that the Testor flat black jar paint is closer to a semigloss than a true flat color.

A semigloss paint is made by mixing a flat paint with a gloss paint. Match the colors as closely as you can unless you want to end up with a different shade. Proportion of gloss to flat will vary depending on the degree of semigloss you want. Start out at about a 50-50 mix and then add more gloss or flat color depending on the degree of semigloss you want. Always make a test after adding more paint. Allow the test paint to dry before making a judgment.

REALISTIC TIRES

Most tires can be made to look more realistic with just the use of some sandpaper. By sanding the tread of a tire, you remove the shine on both vinyl and

Fig. 6-18. Similar to the wire hinge is the HO gauge "barn door" hinge. Bend it like the wire hinge, and it will serve basically the same purpose. Available at most better stocked model railroad hobby shops.

rubberlike tires and give them a much more realistic appearance. This tip is especially effective for racing slicks. (See also Fig. 6-20.)

INSTRUMENT DECALS

Many of the larger scale kits come with decals for their instruments. These add greatly to the realism of a model car. Whenever possible, do not soak the decals off the paper backing and apply them as you normally would. Cut the decals apart (cutting as close to the decal as possible on front mounted decals) and then epoxy them in place. If the dials are made to go behind the instrument openings, leave enough paper around the decals so that you can epoxy the paper to the back of the dial openings.

TAPE RESIDUE

If you leave a model taped together with masking tape for a while, some of the adhesive might remain on the part when the tape is removed. If the tape hasn't fully dried out, most of the adhesive residue can be removed by placing a piece of fresh tape over the residue, pressing it into firm contact, and then just lifting the tape.

This usually will lift the residue, but the technique might need to be repeated several times. Wipe the area with a soft cloth. If this method does not remove the residue, and if the piece is not yet painted, Bare-Metal Plastic Polish will remove most stubborn residue. If you can't use the polish, rub the residue off with a soft cloth as best you can.

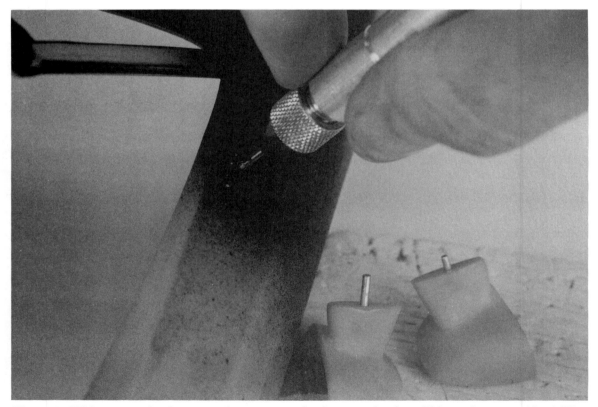

Fig. 6-19. Without mounting lugs, some items are very hard to epoxy in place. This can be corrected by drilling a hole in the piece and epoxying a pin to the hole. Now just drill a hole in the body (or whatever) and epoxy the piece in place.

REMOVING DECALS

If you use Solvaset to remove decals (Fig. 6-22), use it with caution and as a last resort. This procedure could damage the paint, but if the decal is ruining it anyway, it is worth a try. The big problem in this example is that once the decal was off, there was an adhesive residue that was almost impossible to remove. Rubbing the area with Solvaset, soapy detergent water, and wax will usually solve the problem.

At the other end of the decal problem, if you have a decal that will not snuggle down into place, the Solvaset will usually help you here. Use as recommended on the package.

GLUE SPOTS ON CLEAR PARTS

No matter how careful you are or how experienced you might be in building model cars, there will come a time when you get a spot of glue on a clear part. Using epoxy to attach clear parts can just about eliminate this problem. If you do some custom work on the model, however, the clear parts are taped in place while you are working and that leaves them open for glue spots.

If a drop of glue lands on a clear part, carefully get as much off as possible. Use the tip of a knife to remove as much of a drop of tube glue (don't nick the plastic though) or a paper towel for liquid glue (dip one edge into the drop and let the towel soak up the excess glue).

Once you have done all you can to get as much glue off the part, let the glue dry completely. Nothing can be done until the glue is *totally* dry. Once dry, sand the glue spot out with either 400-grit wet sandpaper and then 600-grit sandpaper if the spot is deep or just 600-grit paper if the spot is mainly on the surface of the clear part.

Fig. 6-20. To simulate valve stems, drill a hole in the wheel for a piece of wire. Now cut a short length of wire and file one end flat. Insert this wire in the hole; epoxy in place if necessary. The size of the wire depends on the scale of the model.

When you have finished sanding with the 600-grit paper, the spot should be gone. In its place will be a lot of light scratches. To remove the scratches from sanding and make the part clear again, first rub out the sanding marks with a liquid rubbing compound. Follow this with more rubbing with one of the available plastic polishing kits. This should restore the clear piece. However, the piece will never be as good as new because the sanding will usually cause some distortion. At least the glue spot will be forgotten. (For more tips, see Figs. 6-23 through 6-25).

STRIPPING PAINT FROM PLASTIC

If you ruin a paint job, or if you get an old model with a bad paint job you want to restore, there are several methods that can be used to remove the paint from the plastic.

Not counting the part(s) from which you want to strip the paint, the first item you need is a container for the stripping solution. A plastic shoe box will work fine, but it is on the large side and will require a lot of solution to fill it so that the solution covers the part(s) you want to strip. Any plastic container with a top will work as long as the parts fit in it.

The safest solution for stripping enamel paint is a household cleaner with ammonia. Unfortunately, this will only soak enamel, and it doesn't do it quickly. Soaking time is usually several weeks or more. Some paint, such as a candy color with a silver base, strip easier than others. But for the most part, it takes weeks to strip a car in a cleaner such

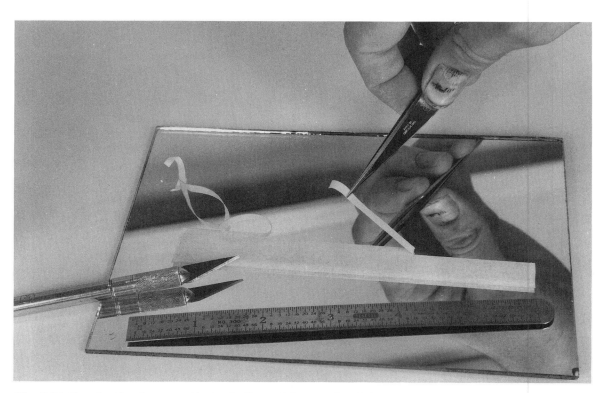

Fig. 6-21. For chopping tops or sectioning bodies, striping tape in all sizes is the best bet. This isn't possible when you have a job requiring a different size strip you can cut the width you need from a piece of masking tape. Cut this tape on a piece of glass.

as Top Job. And some enamel paints don't seem fazed by this solution at all. After a few days of soaking, you should take the car out of the solution and use an old toothbrush to scrub the paint to help loosen it.

Although ammonia-based cleaning solutions will soak enamel paints, they won't touch lacquers at all. Models painted in automotive paints that need to be stripped can be soaked in brake fluid. If you use brake fluid, get the inexpensive kind. There is a brake fluid on the market now that has been specially formulated to eliminate the problem of spilled brake fluid discoloring or removing automotive paint. If the brake fluid container says it is not harmful to a car's finish, don't buy it. It won't soak the paint off the model either.

You must be very careful when you are handling brake fluid, because it will take the paint off anything it touches. The container for soaking the paint off should be covered and made of plastic. The type of paint used will determine how long it needs to be soaked. Check the car every other day and scrub the paint with a brush to speed soaking. A word of warning here. If you have any small cuts on your hand, both the ammonia and the brake fluid will find them.

Brake fluid will work much faster than the ammonia cleaner. While the cleaner might take weeks with enamel paints, the brake fluid might take only days. Freshly bungled enamel paint jobs put right into brake fluid might be ready to paint again within a week—depending on the type of paint.

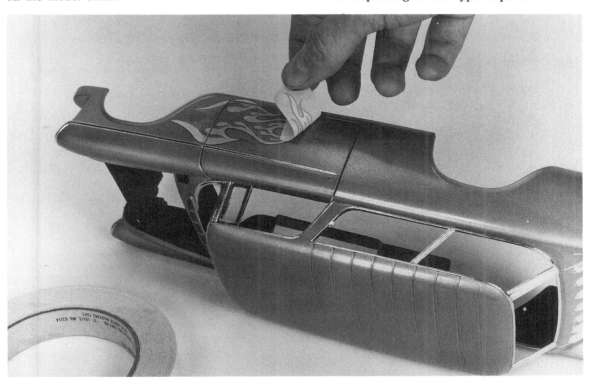

Fig. 6-22. If the decals you applied don't look just right, you can usually remove them by rewetting and pulling. If they have dried a day or two, apply a piece of masking tape to the decal. Remove the tape and the decal often comes with it. You may have to apply the tape several times. If decals are really stubborn, you may have to lay a piece of cloth over the decal and wet it with decal softening solution. Check frequently to make sure the solution isn't harming the surface of the model. Do not let the cloth dry out.

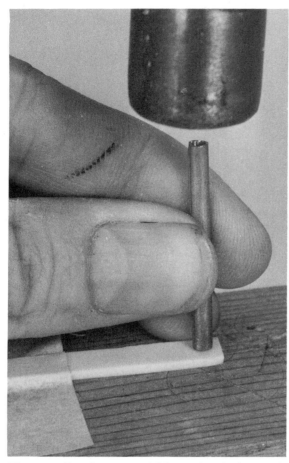

Fig. 6-23. Punches are useful items, but don't come in many sizes. To make a punch, select a piece of brass tubing in the desired size. Using a #11 X-Acto blade, narrow the tube wall so it comes to a chisel edge. As a punch, the brass tube won't last long, but they are easy to make and come in any size for which there is a brass tube.

After you have soaked the paint off, clean off the brake fluid under running water before transferring the parts to soapy water. Clean the parts thoroughly by scrubbing them with a toothbrush. Rinse the parts under running water. This thorough cleaning is especially important with the brake fluid, but both solutions must be completely cleaned off the parts before you try painting them again. After the wash and rinse, I go one step farther. It might

not be necessary, but it doesn't hurt either. Until I paint the parts again, I keep them in a holding tank filled with clean soapy water. These parts are again rinsed under running water and then left to dry before painting.

Before you jump for joy about being able to soak paint off plastic, there is another major problem I haven't mentioned. Either solution will also soak off the body putty you might have applied. This is not much of a problem unless you have customized the car.

REMOVING CHROME PLATING

There are times when you might want to remove the chrome plating from a part. This is especially true if you want the part painted instead of plated. The best solution for soaking the chrome off is an ammonia-based cleaner like Top Job. In most cases, four hours in the solution will remove any trace of chrome from the part. Clean the part as described in the paint removal section.

MURPHY'S LAW

Murphy's law states that if something can go wrong, it will. That is a law all model car builders should know. If you start to think to yourself, "I've got it made now!" just wait a while and Murphy's law will find some way to work itself in. Almost without exception, a model car has to have some problems at some point in its construction.

I have never made a custom in all the years that I have been building models without Murphy's law coming into play. It usually happens at a major point in the construction. In fact, if things go well for too long, Murphy's law is usually just saving itself until you let your guard down. Then it reaches out and grabs you.

Murphy's law will not figure in all the kits you will ever build. Some kits just seem to fall together with no problem. Just don't do too many of this type of kit. You might just be building up to a Murphy's law to end all Murphy's laws! One positive thing you have to admit about Murphy's law, it does keep model car building interesting.

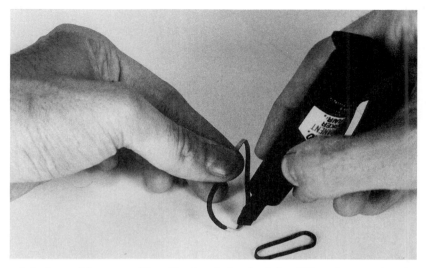

Fig. 6-24. Some of the larger kits come with rubber bands for fan belts. When these are just in a tan color, they can be easily colored to simulate a fan belt by going over them with a permanent black marker.

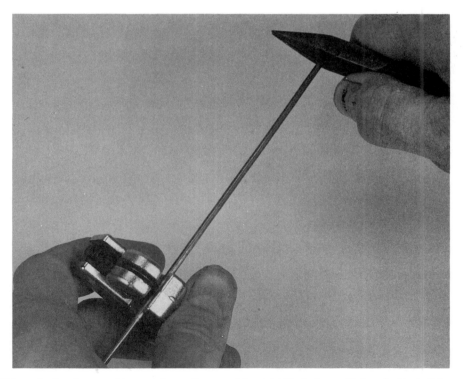

Fig. 6-25. Although aluminum tubing can be easily cut with a #11 blade in an X-Acto knife (roll it on the tubing until you cut through), brass tubing is best cut with a tube cutter. Flatten one end of the tube so you can hold it with a pair of pliers while turning the cutter.

Chapter 7

Displaying Your Models

A model display room is the dream of every model car builder and collector. Unfortunately, that is a dream that comes true for only a few collectors. Still, most collectors do have at least a few of their prize models on display.

SHOW CASES

Displaying most models from 1/16 scale down is made easier by the availability of individual show cases for the model cars. Minicraft Models now produces a display case for 1/16-scale models (Figs. 7-1 and 7-2); these cases were formerly made by Entex. Although it will fit most 1/16-scale model cars, it is not wide enough for all of them. The Minicraft cases do come disassembled and have to be built up before they can be used. After making several tries, I believe epoxy is the best adhesive for assembling this case.

Epoxy the case together according to instructions. To make the case totally dust free, epoxy the seams the same way you filled the seams for the spoilers in Chapter 6. Work on only one surface at a time and wipe the excess epoxy off before it has a chance to set. Do the long seams at the top in at least two separate operations. Go no more than one-third of the way across the top at one time. Do the ends first and then the middle third. Epoxy holds the case together well and allows no dust to get to the model.

Jo-Han makes cases for 1/25- and 1/43-scale cars and 1/72-scale airplanes. Although the one case is meant for airplanes, it can be used to display two to three 1/43-scale cars. It is also very well suited for small model car dioramas. If you have no glassed-in show case or shelves, these Jo-Han Sho-Cases are ideal.

Cases are not the only way to display your models. The ideal way to display the models would be in a glassed-in wall case. Many collectors and builders have wall displays, but few of them are glassed in. Displaying a model of any kind on an open shelf is asking for trouble. These models attract dust, and once a model gets dusty, there is no way to get it really clean. This is especially true for the interiors. The open display of models is to be avoided if it is at all possible.

Fig. 7-1. The large box is the Entex showcase for 1/16-scale models; some 1/25-scale trucks fit this as well. The Jo-Han Sho Case above the Entex (now produced by Minicraft) case is for 1/25-scale models. The Sho Case on the lower left is for 1/72-scale aircraft, and hundreds of other items. The case above the 1/72 case is for 1/43-size model cars.

Fig. 7-2. Using the commercially available show cases a very attractive display of your models can be made up. And while it would be rather costly to outfit a display like this one, if you buy a case every now and then, the expense is distributed over a long period of time. You could also buy two cases each time you finish one model.

Fig. 7-3. An old television and an aquarium converted to show cases. The aquarium need not be one that holds water. The large case on top was manufactured in the 60s and is no longer available. The smaller cases on top come with the die cast cars.

Glassed-in bookcases are another display medium used by many people. The regular store display case is yet another excellent possibility for displaying models, but keep in mind that most store cases are rear loading. In a house, that could create problems. Older watch display cases are used by many collectors to display a few models, and they do make excellent cases for the most part.

AQUARIUMS AND CABINETS

Still another excellent display case is a fish aquarium (Fig. 7-3). These come in many sizes (listed in gallons) and they can be used for the display of larger models.

Yet another type of display cabinet can be made from an old cabinet-model television set. Older style televisions are best, because many had a flat glass front to them. These sets are also the easiest to convert. To convert a television to a display cabinet, first gut the electronics portion of the set. That is not as easy as it sounds. Even after the set is unplugged, there are still parts that could zap you if you touched them. If you gut the TV yourself, be careful and treat everything with the greatest respect.

Unplug the television and let it set for several weeks. Remove the back of the set and locate the transformer. The transformer is the rectangular black metal box on top of the chassis. Short all of the red wires and the red and yellow striped wires coming from the transformer. To short the wires, hold onto the plastic portion of a screwdriver while short-circuiting any exposed, bare wire to the metal chassis with the metal rod of the screwdriver. Do not touch the transformer with any part of your body. In addition, short the cap on top of the high-voltage tubes to the chassis using the same technique. The high-voltage tubes are located in a separate compartment. Be very careful how you handle the picture tube.

Once the set is gutted, the first step is to add a glass front. Even if the set has a flat glass front, it will probably need to be replaced. Most of these sets have tinted glass. Thin window glass will work as a replacement. Either have it cut to size or cut it yourself to fit the opening in the cabinet. If the television didn't come with a flat glass front, you will have to add one. You should also make it so that the glass is removable from the front. This can usually be done by adding a screw-in strip across the top of the cabinet to hold the glass in place.

Once you have a glass front that you can remove when you want to change models, decide if you also want to add any glass shelves to the cabinet. Before you add a shelf, however, completely cover the inside of the cabinet with poster board or paneling. To add a shelf, use half round wood molding to hold it in place.

As a final feature, think about adding a light to show off the models. Fluorescent is preferable because of the amount of heat other lights put out.

Appendix A

Sources

This section contains addresses, arranged in alphabetical order, of manufacturers, suppliers, dealers (kits and die-cast models, old and new), and cottage industry producers. When writing any of the people or firms listed, send them a self-addressed stamped envelope (SASE), #10 business envelope preferred, to obtain information on a specific product, or the cost of their current catalogs; catalogs are not free from many dealers anymore. If you are requesting specific information on product availability, do be specific, listing catalog numbers when possible. Do not expect a reply if you don't include an SASE. For foreign addresses, include the self-addressed envelope, but don't apply domestic stamps. In these cases, include at least two International Reply Coupons, available at Post Offices. The person who receives these IRCs can then trade them in for stamps to send you the information you requested.

Because new companies and dealers are always coming along while established firms and dealers are sometimes going out of business or just changing addresses, keeping the Sources list up to date is diffi-cult. I will try to keep this list up to date with new companies, new addresses for established companies, and lists of those no longer doing business. This list will be available by writing me through *Model Car Journal*, P.O. Box 154135, Irving, TX 75015-4135. Please address envelopes to Book Revisions, include an SASE, and 20¢ for copy costs, to receive the latest deletions and additions.

The following list of addresses does not constitute an endorsement by either the author or TAB BOOKS, Inc.

Accent Models, Inc.
P.O. Box 295
Denville, NJ 07834
(Dealer: new die-cast, kits, some promos)

Acrylic Creations, Inc.
500 Winfred
Lansing, MI 48917
(Acrylic display cases, all sizes)

Applegate & Applegate
P.O. Box 1
Annville, PA 17003
(Original auto literature, paint charts, factory photos)

The Attic Fanatic
9017 Reseda Blvd.
Northridge, CA 91324
(Dealer: old Corgi, Dinky, Matchbox, plastic kits, promos)

Autobooks Etc.
3524 W. Magnolia Blvd.
Burbank, CA 91505
(Old and new auto books and magazines)

Autofanatics Ltd.
P.O. Box 1091
Studio City, CA 91604
(Dealer: new die-cast and kits in all scales, promos)

Automobiles In Scale
6822 Foxborough Ct.
Yorba Linda, CA 92686
(Dealer: kits, books, detail items)

Auto-Mobilia
P.O. Box 247
Denton, NC 27239
(Dealer: model cars and magazines)

Automobilia
44 Glendale Rd.
P.O. Box 38
Park Ridge, NJ 07656
(Dealer: die-cast, pewter, and tin cars)

Auto Motif, Inc.
2968 Atlanta Rd.
Smyrna, GA 30080
(Dealer: kits, die-cast, supplies, automobile)

Auto Motif Imports & Museum
P.O. Box 5738
Woodland Park, CO 80866
(Dealer: new and old die-cast)

Automotive Memorables
650 Kenmore Blvd.
Akron, OH 44314
(Dealer: model cars, auto literature, magazines, etc.)

Automotive Miniatures and Accessories
Rt. 3, Box 1578
Odessa, FL 33556
(Cottage manufacturer and dealer: parts and detail items of all types)

Autophile
1685 Bayview Ave.
Toronto, Ontario
Canada M4G 3C1
(Dealer: 1/43-models, books, and magazines)

Auto Replicas Ltd.
23, Bailey Crescent
Poole
Dorset, BH15 3EZ
England
(Manufacturer white-metal kits)

Auto World
701 N. Keyser Ave.
Scranton, PA 18508
(Dealer since 1959: full line, kits, supplies, books, etc.)

Badger Air Brush Co.
9128 Belmont Ave.
Franklin Park, IL 60131

Bare-Metal Foil Co.
P.O. Box 82
Farmington, MI 48024

Bargains Galore
163 W. LaHabra Blvd.
LaHabra, CA 90631
(Dealer: plastic kits old and new)

Don Berry
5316 Skeeswood Dr.
Kearns, UT 84118
(Manufacturer: white-metal parts for trucks)

Bob Blum
8 Leto Rd.
Albany, NY 12203
(Dealer: die-cast Tomy Pocket Cars)

Mody K. Boatright
629 Santa Monica
Corpus Christi, TX 78411
(Dealer: auto literature, some models)

Bob's Hobbies
344 N. 15th, 6C
Pocatello, ID 83201
(Dealer: old truck kits, semi-scratchbuilt trailer conversions)

Booth Hobbies
596 Concession St.
Hamilton, Ontario
Canada L8V 1B3
(Dealer)

B P Industries
P.O. Box 176
Canby, OR 97013
(Manufacturer: wood boxes for hobbiests)

Brasilia Press
P.O. Box 2023
Elkhart, IN 46515
(Wholesale importer 1/43-models, promo, and kit guide)

Brooklin Models
Unit 3, Pinesway Industrial Estate
Ivo Peters Rd.
Bath, Avon
England BA2 3QS
(Manufacturer: 1/43-white-metal models)

William E. Buckingham
7335 W. 109 Place
Worth, IL 60482
(Dealer: old kits and promos)

Fred Cady Design
P.O. Box 576
Mount Prospect, IL 60056
(Manufacturer: decals for all types of model cars)

Caltronics Lab
P.O. Box 36356
Los Angeles, CA 90036-0356
(Very small bolts, taps, dies, drills, etc.)

Canuck Auto Replicas
P.O. Box 656
Orleans, Ontario
Canada K1C 3V9
(Manufacturer: license plates and body filler, Bonneville tires/wheel discs, kits)

Richard Carlson Productions
(address in *Model Car Journal*)
(Manufacturer: resin models, parts, etc.)

Robert Cerame
517 Pelican Bay Dr.
Daytona Beach, FL 32019
(Dealer: promos and old 1/25-kits)

CHROME +
5865 Bach St.
Brossard, Quebec
Canada J4Z 2G3
(Chrome and gold plating of plastic parts, replacement parts)

Classic Motorbooks
P.O. Box 1
Osceola, WI 54020
(Large catalog of car and model car books)

Col Grey Components
P.O. Box 1052
Ivanhoe 3079
Victoria, Australia
(Manufacturer: 1/25- and 1/16-scale truck parts of all types)

Collectors Toys & Hobbies
40 W. 11th Ave.
York, PA 17404
(Dealer: old and new, plastic models, die-cast, toys)

Con-Cor International
1025 Industrial Dr.
Bensenville, IL 60106-1297
(Importer/mfg: HO and smaller cars and trucks, railroad scenery)

John A. Conde
1340 Fieldway Dr.
Bloomfield Hills, MI 48013
(Dealer: auto literature)

Connoissuer Motorbooks
48 E. 50th St. (3rd Floor)
New York, NY 10022
(Dealer: auto books and magazines)

Copy Cars
P.O. Box 481
Tustin, CA 92681
(Dealer: mostly 1/43-die-cast and plastic cars)

Corgi Sales Ltd.
Kingsway, Swansea Industrial Estate
Forestfach, Swansea
England SA5 4EL
(Manufacturer: die-cast cars and trucks/all vintages)

Larry Cornell
5804 Ironwood St.
San Bernardino, CA 92404
(Dealer: 1/25-scale, promos and old kits)

C&P Auto Modelling Supplies
P.O. Box 41
Terang, 3264
Victoria Australia
(Dealer: kits, supplies; manufacturer and distributor: model car and truck parts)

Crank 'En Hope Publications
461 Sloan Alley
Blairsville, PA 15717
(Dealer: discounted auto books)

Creations Unlimited
2939 Montreat Dr., NE
Grand Rapids, MI 49505
(Flex-I-File, epoxy putty, and other finishing materials, tools)

Dale Dannefer
P.O. Box 29002
Rochester, NY 14627
(Dealer: Stahlberg and other European promos, 1/43-models, U.S. promos)

D and D Hobby
#3 Charles St.
Carnegie, PA 15106
(Detailing products for 1/25-scale cars and trucks)

Herb Deeks Models
1516 E. Santa Ana St.
Anaheim, CA 92805
(Manufacturer: wide range of resin, acid etched, and white-metal parts and kits)

Der Alt Mann Of Auto's
4524 LuAnn Ave.
Toledo, OH 43623
(Dealer: Pirate Models, die-cast replacement parts, die-cast restoration)

Discount Book Co.
P.O. Box 3150
San Rafael, CA 94912-3150
(Dealer: auto books)

D & J Enterprises
738 Main St.
Neenah, WI 54956
(1/25-1/24 detail items for cars and trucks, fuzzy dice)

D & L Corvette Miniatures
191 Sheffield Dr.
Danville, IN 46122
(Dealer: Corvette models and related items)

John R. Dragich Collectible Auto Literature
1500 93rd Lane, NE
Minneapolis, MN 55434

Dupli-Color Products Co.
1601 Nicolas Blvd.
Elk Grove Village, IL 60007-5677
(Manufacturer: automotive paints)

Enchantment Land Coachbuilders
7039 Katchina Ct.
Tucson, AZ 85715
(¹⁄₄₃-conversions, die-cast restoration, limited productions)

ENCO Models
Unit 28, Alfric Square
Woodston
Peterborough
England PE2 0JP
(Manufacturer: ¹⁄₄₃-models plus wheel sets)

Ertl AMT/MPC/Esci
Highways 136 & 20
Dyersville, IA 52040

Euro-Truck
P.O. Box 472
Post Office Champlain
LaSalle, Quebec
Canada H8P 2N7
(Dealer: hard-to-find truck kits from Europe)

Form & Functon
P.O. Box 14037
Lenexa, KS 66215
(Dealer: kits, literature, etc.)

Formula 1
5 Keane Ave.
Islington, Ontario
Canada M9B 2B6
(Dealer: car kits, all types and scales)

Foto-Cut
P.O. Box 120
Erieville, NY 13061
(Manufacturer: acid etched parts of all types)

Franklin's Diecast Miniatures, Inc.
1008 Doon Village Rd.
Kitchner, Ontario
Canada N2P 1A5
(Dealer: die-cast, specializing in Matchbox, Lledo, and Corgi)

Robert Gallarado
658 Cornell Dr.
Santa Paula, CA 93060
(Dealer/collector: older models)

Garage Scenes/R&B Video
19088 Santa Maria Ave.
Castro Valley, CA 94546
(Manufacturer: parts and diorama items, model meet and how-to videos)

William E. Gebhard
228 E. Rosedale Ave.
Milwaukee, WI 53207
(Manufacturer: vacuum formed Indy race car bodies)

Get It On Paper
185 Maple St.
Islip, NY 11751
(Dealer: auto literature, model ads)

Gilltraps
Box 128
Palm Beach, Q. 4221
Australia
(Dealer: old and new models)

F.P. Gortsema
7 Briarwood Lane
Pleasantville, NY 10570
(Manufacturer: truck conversion kits)

C.D. Gough
2718 1358 Street
Surry, B.C.
Canada V3W 7M5
(Multiview sheets of race cars for correct decal placements)

Grandpa's Attic
112 E. Washington St.
Goshen, IN 46526
(Dealer: die-cast, promos, Matchbox, auto literature)

Grand Prix Models
176 Watling St.
Radlett,
Herts.
England WD7 7NQ
*(Dealer: die-cast all scales; manufacturer:
⅟₄₃-models)*

Group 43 Auto Miniatures
7 Wadsworth St.
Danvers, MA 01923
(Dealer: ⅟₄₃-scale models and kits)

Stanley T. Grzybowski
11011 Hupp St.
Warren, MI 48089
(⅟₂₄-diorama accessories)

Hamilton's
P.O. Box 932
Bedford, VA 24523
*(Dealer: Matchbox size die-casts from all manufac-
turers)*

Steve Hayward
2313 Mulberry Ct.
Champaign, IL 61821
(Resin parts for stock car racers, etc.)

John Heyer
165 Kemball Ave.
Staten Island, NY 10314
(Manufacturer: resin bodies, kits and parts)

Hobby Heaven
P.O. Box 3229
Grand Rapids, MI 49501
(Dealer: old and new kits, cottage produced parts)

Hobby Surplus Sales
287 Main St.
P.O. Box 2170
New Britain CT 06050
(Dealer: kits, die-cast, supplies, tools, misc.)

Hobbytown
P.O. Box 325
Seekonk, MA 02771
(Dealer: fire models, truck kits and parts, die-cast)

Illini Replica Conversions
24808 S. 88th Ave.
Frankfort, IL 60423
*(Manufacturer: resin big rig truck and pickup con-
versions, and parts)*

International Hobby Supply
P.O. Box 426
Woodland Hills, CA 91365
*(Importer: wide range of plastic and domestic kits,
supplies, tools)*

Ivers Engineering
P.O. Box 361
Brewer, MA 04412
(Manufacturer: HO white-metal truck kits)

Jerry's Automotive Miniatures
2229 Judy
Odessa, TX 79764
(Dealer: new and old kits)

Jielge Models
B.P. No. 21,
74120 Megeve
France
*(Manufacturer: ⅟₄₃-models, plus promotionals and
models in all scales)*

Jo-Han Models, Inc.
17255 Moran Ave.
Detroit, MI 48212

Don Johansen
2040 Tremont Ave.
Davenport, IA 52803
(Dealer: old kits and promos)

John's Mail Order Models
P.O. Box 892
Drumheller, Alberta
Canada T0J 0Y0
*(Manufacturer and dealer: resin parts, dealer in old
kits)*

The Jones Collection
261 Heagle Crescent
Edmonton, Alberta
Canada T6J 1W2
(Blueprints of old trucks for scratchbuilders)

Jordan Products
P.O. Box 644
Brighton, MI 48116
(Manufacturer: plastic HO scale cars and trucks of high detail)

J.R. Enterprises
P.O. Box 561
Ridgewood, NJ 07451
(1/24-scale diorama material)

Kastpro
P.O. Box 7018
Van Nuys, CA 91409-7018
(Resin casting supplies, resin casting video how-to)

Ken's Kustom Kar Supply
P.O. Box 85
Fremont, OH 43420
(Detailing supplies, including Fuzzi-Fur)

Knapico
6 Lake Christopher Ct.
Rockville, MD 20853
(Dealer: sports car models, especially Ferrari and Porsche)

Krasel Industries, Inc.
P.O. Box 11950
Costa Mesa, CA 92627
(Manufacturer: supplies and material for hobby)

Lambert Ley Street Ltd.
309 Ley St.
Ilford
Essex
England IG1 4AA
(Dealer: die-cast, kits in all materials)

William J. Landis, Inc.
1841 Ashton Dr.
Lebanon, PA 17042
(Manufacturer: parts; dealer: promos, kits, custom painting)

Ed Leo California Decals
P.O. Box 7101
Oakland, CA 94601
(Decals for California license plates)

Lilliput Motor Car Co.
P.O. Box 156
Clarksburg, NJ 08510
(Dealer: mostly 1/43-models, plus auto literature, magazines, etc.)

Lindberg Products, Inc.
940 North Shore Dr.
Lake Bluff, IL 60044

LMG Enterprises
1627 S. 26th St.
Sheboygan, WI 53081
(Scratchbuilding and superdetailing parts and supplies, diorama items)

Mac Lay Automobiles
337 Harold Ave.
Leonia, NJ 07605
(Dealer: die-casts, conversions, and master models for limited production)

Gary MacNorius
14770 N.W. Garden Dr.
Miami, FL 33168
(Dealer: promos and European 1/43-models)

Main Street Hobby and Toy
3624 Main St.
Kansas City, MO 64111
(Dealer: kits, die-cast, old and new)

Manywell Limited
20 Godfries Close
Tewin, Welyn
Herts.
England AL6 0LQ
(Export agent for Matchbox kits)

Rick Manz
15216 N. 30th Dr.
Phoenix, AZ 85023
(Manufacturer: 1/25-truck tractor conversion kits)

Marque Products
P.O. Box 2935
Seal Beach, CA 90740-1935
(Dealer: die-cast and plastic; models and kits; magazines and books)

Marsh Models
25 St. Mary's Road
New Romney, Kent
England TN28 8JG
(Manufacturer: 1/43-kits and built models in white metal)

Master Creations
P.O. Box 1378
Chino Valley, AZ 86323
(HO vehicles, railroad detail parts)

Dick McKnight
P.O. Box 375
Tully, NY 13159
(Dealer: auto literature)

Merkel Model Car Company
P.O. Box 689
Franklin Park, IL 60131
(Dealer: old and new kits, promos, die-cast etc.)

Micro Mark
340 Snyder Ave.
Berkeley Hts., NJ 07922
(Small hand tools of all types)

Mikansue
15 Bell Lane
Eton Wick
Windsor, Berks
England SL4 6LQ
(Manufacturer: white-metal models and kits)

Milano 43/Tron Kits
c/o Gary David
P.O. Box 39
Macedonia, OH 44056
(U.S. connection for Tron kits and TSSK catalog)

Milano 43
Via Boeri, 11
20141 Milano
Italy
(Manufacturer: Tron kits, dealer in many other models, mostly 1/43)

Milepost 501 Hobbies
16124 E. Old Valley Blvd.
LaPuente, CA 91744
(Manufacturer: HO truck trailers)

Milestone Miniatures Inc.
136-41A Jewel Ave.
Flushing, NY 11367
(Manufacturer: 1/25-resin kits)

S.C. Miller
P.O. Drawer J
Dublin, VA 24084
(Manufacturer: large series of resin kits)

Miniature Auto Sales, Inc.
P.O. Box 264902
Bethlehem, CT 06751
(Dealer: old and new die-cast)

Miniature Cars USA
P.O. Box 221
Bernardsville, NJ 07924
(Dealer: die-cast and plastic; models and kits; promos, old and new; foreign magazines)

Miniature Machine Models
P.O. Box 597544
Chicago, IL 60659
(Dealer: domestic and foreign kits)

Mini-Auto Emporium
14 Grenfell Crescent, Unit 2
Nepean, Ontario
Canada K2G 0G2
(Dealer and manufacturer: 1/43-U.S. and racing cars)

Minicraft Models, Inc.
1510 West 228th St.
Torrance, CA 90510
(Manufacturer/importer: plastic kits)

Mini Exotics
936 Pearce Portal Dr.
P.O. Box 8014
Blain, WI 98230
(Manufacturer: resin parts and diorama items)

Mini Grid
4461 Highway #7
Unionville, Ontario
Canada L3R 1M1
(Dealer: mostly 1/43-scale models, die-cast and resin)

Mini-Marque 43
The Old Farm House
Robin Hood Way
Winnersh, Nr. Reading
England RG11 5JJ
(Manufacturer: assembled 1/43-U.S. models)

Model Auto
10885 Katy Fwy., Suite 22
Houston, TX 77079
(Dealer: old promos and kits)

ModelAuto
P.O. Box MT1
Leeds,
West Yorkshire
England LS17 6TA
(Dealer/manufacturer: die-cast and resin kits and models)

Model Car Masterpieces
1525 W. MacArthur Blvd., #20
Costa Mesa, CA 92626
(Dealer: 1/43-resin and white-metal kits; plus tools and supplies)

Model Car and Parts
204 W. 71 Hwy
Savannah, MO 64485
(Manufacturer: resin bodies and parts)

The Model Car Shop
28 Arthur Ave.
Blue Point, NY 11715
(Dealer: 1/43-specialty models)

Model Empire
10500 W. Loomis Rd.
Franklin, WI 53132-9617
(Dealer: old and new kits, promos, die-cast, supplies, etc.)

The Modelhaus
3321 Ferris Dr.
Decatur, IL 62521
(Manufacturer: 1/25-scale resin conversion kits, parts, etc., very high quality)

Modellautos—Gestern + Heute
Giselastr. 8
D-8000 Munchen 40,
West Germany
(Dealer: all types of model cars, HO to 1/24)

Model Rectifier Corp.
2500 Woodbridge Ave.
Edison, NJ 08817
(Importer/manufacturer: Tamiya kits)

The Model Shop
W7867 County Z
Onalaska, WI 54650
(Dealer: old and new kits, supplies, tools)

Model Store House
8580 Gaines Ave.
Orangevale, CA 95662
(Dealer: kits, scratchbuilding and detailing supplies)

Model Truck & Fire Apparatus Co.
P.O. Box 624
Irvington, NJ 07111
(Manufacturer: model truck parts, new name for AIM)

Monogram Models, Inc.
8601 Waukegan Rd.
Morton Grove, IL 60053

Motor Cities Publishing Co.
10405 Rushton Rd.
South Lyon, MI 48178
(Publisher of Ford A and early V-8 books, excellent for detailing models)

Motor City U.S.A.
P.O. Box 435
Encino, CA 91436
(Manufacturer: 1/43-scale white-metal models)

Motorsports Miniatures
4157 Grand Ave. S.
Minneapolis, MN 55409
(Dealer: kits and die-cast; manufacturer: resin conversion bodies for 1/25-kits)

Motorsports Miniatures
82 Wall St., Suite 1105
New York, NY 10005
(Dealer: 1/43-white-metal models and kits)

MPB Detail Products
11418 Bullis Rd.
Marilla, NY 14102
(Manufacturer: conversion parts in resin and plastic)

Mr. Fury Miniature Motors
7395 162nd St. West
Rosemount, MN 55068
(Dealer: promos, specializing in Corvette)

MSC Model Products
Division Of Millenium Sales Corp.
22 South Balsam St.
Lakewood, CO 80226
(Manufacturer/dealer: detailing supplies; cottage industry parts, etc.)

Munchkin Motors
20 Westford Rd.
P.O. Box 266
Eastford, CT 06242
(Dealer: die-cast models, plastic kits)

Nathan's Studio
College Farm
High Street
Pulloxhill, Beds.
England MK45 5HB
(Dealer: Ferrari models and accessories)

Dr. Jesse Nolph
510 S. 106th St.
Tacoma, WA 98444
(Dealer: promos and kits)

Northwest Short Line
P.O. Box 423
Seattle, WA 98111
(Small bulbs, tools, railroad items)

Nostalgia Enterprises
P.O. Box 300
Lockport, NY 14094
(Dealer: old kits and toys, figure kits)

The Old Toy Box
Edgewood Dr. Ext.
P.O. Box 338
Transfer, PA 16154
(Dealer: die-cast cars, trucks, construction, old toys)

Paasche Airbrush Co.
7440 W. Lawrence Ave.
Harwood Hts., IL 60656

Pactra Hobby
P.O. Box 280
Upland, CA 91786
(Manufacturer: hobby paints and finishing supplies)

Parts By Parks
1103 E. State St.
Marshalltown, IA 50158
(Manufacturer: aluminum detailing parts, wheel covers, etc.)

Joe Passamano
506 W. Phillips Ct.
Grand Prairie, TX 75051
(Dealer: new die-cast)

Paul's Hobby Shop
569 North 1st East
Tremonton, UT 84337
(Dealer: old and new car and truck kits, supplies)

Pavan's Pontiacs/Delawanna Hobby
200 Rutherford Blvd.
Clifton, NJ 07014
(Dealer: Pontiac models specialty, kits, some promos, parts)

Barry Payne
102 Circle Dr.
Fairborn, OH 45324
(Dealer: model cars, custom builder)

Performance Poster Co.
3 Stewart Ct.
Denville, NJ 07834
(Excellent and inexpensive posters)

David Peters' Racing Replicas
7443 Indiana Ave.
Riverside, CA 92504
(Manufacturer: resin bodies for funny cars/pro stock)

Photo-Rific
10815 S.W. 57th Ave.
Portland, OR 97219
(Dealer: die-cast/resin kits and models, pins, shirts, posters)

Pinecrest Scale Models
161 Maple Ln.
Jamestown, PA 16134
(Manufacturer: resin conversion kits for trucks)

Pit Stop Shoppe
P.O. Box 190062
Burton, MI 48519
(Dealer: die-cast and Banthrico banks)

Ronn Pittman
1024 Raddant Rd.
Batavia, IL 60510
(Dealer: US promos and kits, trucks)

Plastruct, Inc.
1020 S. Wallace Place
City Of Industry, CA 91748
(Manufacturer: plastic parts, shapes, sheets, tubes, landscape material)

Polk's Modelcraft Hobbies, Inc.
346 Bergen Ave.
Jersey City, NJ 07304
(Dealer: die-cast and plastic kits, white metal, etc.)

Portman Hobby Distributors
851 Washington St.
Peekskill, NY 10566
(Manufacturer/distributor: HO scale white-metal kits)

Precision Miniatures
1539 Monrovia Ave., Suite 20
Newport Beach, CA 92663
(Manufacturer: 1/43-white metal models)

Precision Scale Co., Inc.
1120-A Gum Ave.
Woodland, CA 95695-1262
(Small light bulbs and many detailing items)

The Putty Thrower
1348 Longdale Dr.
Sandy, UT 84092
(Manufacturer: Scale Scripts®, parts and detailing items of many types)

RCB Cars
P.O. Box 222
Lakeview, CA 92353
(Manufacturer: plaster-cast cars in HO scale)

Rees Precision Miniatures/RPM
2074 Westbranch Rd.
Grove City, OH 43123
(Manufacturer: resin parts for Oldsmobiles)

Replica & Miniatures Company of MD
7479-D Furnace Branch Rd.
Glen Burnie, MD 21061
(Manufacturer: parts and engine kits, decals, acid etched parts, 1/32-tractors)

Revell, Inc.
363 N. Third Ave.
Des Plaines, IL 60016

Revere Auto Miniatures
412 Revere Beach Pky.
Revere, MA 02151
(Dealer: 1/43-models and kits)

Ridgefield Hobby
508 Broad Ave.
Ridgefield, NJ 07657
(Dealer: plastic kits, old and new)

Riverside Hobbies
5681(A) Freeport Blvd.
Sacramento, CA 95822
(Dealer: foreign and domestic plastic kits and supplies; no catalog)

Vince Rogalio
1 Mechanic St.
Troy, NY 12180
(Dealer: kits, magazines, literature)

Alan W. Royer
5732 Aloha Ave.
Knoxville, TN 37921
(Manufacturer: fiberglass accessories and conversion kits for trucks)

R&R Vacuum Craft
8324 Calkins Rd.
Flint, MI 48532
(Manufacturer: vacuum formed up tops, convertible boots, fender scoops, etc.)

San Antonio Hobby Shop, Inc.
2550 W. El Camino
Mt. View, CA 94040
(Dealer: model kits)

Satellite City
P.O. Box 836
Simi, CA 93065
(Manufacturer: adhesives, Hot Stuff and Super T superglues)

Mark Savage
209 Campbell Ave.
Butler, PA 16001
(Manufacturer: detailing parts, wheels, tires, for trucks)

Sayre Hobby Shop
517 South Keystone Ave.
Sayre, PA 18840
(Dealer: new and old kits, cars and trucks)

Scale Auto Replicas
3951 June St.
San Bernardino, CA 92405
(Manufacturer: resin conversion bodies, parts)

Scale Dreams
17922 Gothard, Unit B8
Huntington Beach, CA 92647
(Manufacturer: high-quality limited production 1/25-scale cars)

Scale Equipment Ltd.
P.O. Box 10084
Bradenton, FL 34282
(Manufacturer: diorama/garage parts)

Scale Models
P.O. Box 327
Dyersville, IA 52040
(Manufacturer: collectors farm tractors, and old Hubley/Gabriel die-cast kits)

Scale Model Technical Service (SMTS)
Unit 6, Orchidbrook Industrial Estates
Brunel Road,
Hastings, Sussex
England TN38 9RT
(Manufacturer: white-metal models and kits, complete manufacturing service)

Scale Scenes
Division of Circuitron
P.O. Box 322
Riverside, IL 60546
(Manufacturer: electronics for hobbyist/diorama items)

Scale Signs, Inc.
43027 Ryegate
Canton, MI 48187
(Traffic signs for dioramas)

Scale Sports
1193 Country Highlands Dr.
Hubertus, WI 53033
(Detail Master acid etched items, detailing supplies)

Shabo Scale
2416 N. 66th St.
Wauwatosa, WI 53213
(Decal lettering for tires, whitewall paint, stripes, etc.)

Sherriff's Mini-Cars
P.O. Box 259
Buulkham Hills,
NSW
Australia 2153
(Dealer: die-cast, plastic kits, old and new)

Rick Shnitzler
P.O. Box 521
Narberth, PA 19072
(Dealer: auto literature, paint chips)

Sinclair's Auto Miniatures
P.O. Box 8403
Erie, PA 16505
(The original U.S. die-cast dealer: current die-casts and Pocher kits)

Bob Smith
62 West Ave.
Fairport, NY 14450
(Dealer: mostly old 1/43)

Merrill Smith Co.
Miniature Motors Division
12634 Angling Rd.
Edinboro, PA 16412
(Dealer: mostly 1/43-die-cast)

SNJ Model Products
P.O. Box 28024
Sacramento, CA 95828
(Spray metal products, natural finish, can use masking tape over it)

Somerville Models
Westfield House
104 High Street
Billinghay, Lincoln
England LN4 4ED
(Manufacturer: 1/43-white metal models)

Sportcraft
7511 E. Victoria Dr.
Laingsburg, MI 48848
(Dealer: Porsche and VW models of all types)

The Squadron
1115 Crowley Dr.
Carrollton, TX 75011-5010
(Dealer: die-cast, plastic kits, imports and domestic)

S & S Specialties
2005 Gettysburg Pl.
Bedford, TX 76022
(Many detailing items, acid etched parts)

Star Bronze
P.O. Box 2206
Alliance, OH 44601
(Zip Strip and paints)

The Testor Corp.
620 Buckbee St.
Rockford, IL 61108
(Paints and import kits)

Clark Theilmann
7391 Melody Dr.
Minneapolis, MN 55432
(Dealer: old Gabriel and Hubley die-cast kits)

TKM Models
P.O. Box 57235
Oklahoma City, OK 73157
(Manufacturer: resin car kits in 1/25 - 1/24-scale)

Toys For Collectors
P.O. Box 1406
Attleboro Falls, MA 02763
(Dealer: die-cast models, all types and scales)

Uptown Automotive
P.O. Box 111
New Hartford, NY 13413
(Dealer: domestic and foreign, old and new, kits and promos)

Utah Pacific
P.O. Box 8174
Salt Lake City, UT 84108
(Small bulbs, railroad castings)

Valley Plaza Hobbies
12160 Hamlin St.
North Hollywood, CA 91606
(Dealer: import plastic kits, resin and white-metal models, accessories, books)

Verlinden Productions
25 Cross Keys Center
Florissant, MO 63033
(Dealer: wide selection cottage industry type parts, supplies)

Vintage Motorbooks
42 N.W. Wallula
Gresham, OR 97030
(Dealer: books, especially out-of-print books)

Waldron Model Products
P.O. Box 431
Merlin, OR 97532
(Manufacturer: acid etched seat belt hardware)

Walker Model Services
5235 Farrar Ct.
Downers Grove, IL 60615
(Manufacturer: HO white metal trucks, trailers, parts)

Wm. K. Walthers, Inc.
5601 W. Florist Ave.
Milwaukee, WI 53218
(Manufacturer: HO models, deals in all manner of small scale vehicles, parts, etc.)

Weber's Nostalgia Supermarket
1121 S. Main St.
Ft. Worth, TX 76104
(Dealer: die-casts, all types of auto related items)

Ted Weems
3008 Phyllis
Dallas, TX 75234
(Dealer: promos, magazines, auto literature)

Wheat's Nostalgia
467-C Baldwin Rd.
Pittsburgh, PA 15205
(Dealer: promos, ¹⁄₂₅-kits, related model items)

Wheels Model Cars
Rockbear
Exeter
Devon
England EX5 2ED
(Dealer: mostly ¹⁄₄₃-models, die-cast, resin, white metal)

John Wimble
1407 Stoneycreek Dr.
Richmond, VA 23233
(Dealer: auto literature—postwar)

Woodland Scenes
P.O. Box 98
Linn Creek, MO 65052
(Manufacturer: scenery, dry transfers, PineCar Racer®)

X-EL Products
P.O. Box 34666
Detroit, MI 48234
(Dealer: Jo-Han kits and reissue promos)

Bob Zetterman
7131 Pierce St.
Arvada, CO 80003
(Dealer: promos and kits)

George Zurowski
20 Bradish Ln.
Bayshore, NY 11706
(Dealer: kits, especially large scale)

Appendix B

Magazines

The first section of this Appendix lists magazines the model car builder and collector should find of interest. Magazines listed feature a model column; others are model car magazines being produced as this is written. Send the magazines a SASE with your request for current subscription rates.

Car Collector
8601 Dunwoody Place, Suite 144
Atlanta, GA 30338
(Tries for six model features a year)

Collectible Automobile
Publications International, Ltd.
7373 N. Cicero Ave.
Lincolnwood, IL 60646
(Full color magazine, model column)

Corvette Fever
3816 Industry Blvd.
Lakeland, FL 33811

Four Small Wheels
176 Watling Street
Radlett,
Herts.
England WD7 7NQ
(Extension of Grand Prix Models, mostly die-cast models and kits)

Kit Collectors Clearinghouse
3213 Hardy Dr.
Edmond, OK 73013
(Covers all types of plastic kits, buy/sell section)

Model Auto Review
P.O. Box MT1
Leeds
England LS17 6TA
(Mainly covers 1/43, 1/50, 1/87, as well as other scales)

Model Car Journal
P.O. Box 154135
Irving, TX 75015-4135
(Covers all aspects of the static model car hobby, new models to collectors items)

Pit Road
Lypiatt Cottage
Miserden
Stroud, Glos.
England GL6 7JB
(Covers scale racing models)

Scale Auto Enthusiast
5918 W. North Ave.
Milwaukee, WI 53208
(Covers all aspects of static model cars and trucks)

Small Motor News
40 Fornof Ln.
Pittsburgh, PA 15212
(Old toys, trucks, and vehicles)

Street Rodder
2145 W. LaPalma Ave.
Anaheim, CA 92801-1785

Traders Horn
1903 Schoettler Valley
Chesterfield, MO 63017
(Publication for buy, sell, wanted listings)

Vette Vues Magazine
Drawer A
Sandy Springs, GA 30328

The following magazines generally do not have model car features in them. They are listed because they are either excellent sources for buying or selling model cars, or their real car features offer exceptional coverage, helpful in detailing models of the cars they feature.

It should be noted many of the real car magazines in the late '50s and early '60s featured model cars. *Rod & Custom* featured models in most issues well into the '60s. Model features can also be found in *Car Craft*, *Custom Craft*, and *'50s Motor Trend*.

Cars & Parts
P.O. Box 482
Sidney, OH 45365
(Also produce annuals that are highly recommended, sometimes these feature model cars)

Hemmings Motor News
P.O. Box 100
Bennington, VT 05201
(Giant magazine, mostly ads)

Muscle Car Review
P.O. Drawer 7157
Lakeland, FL 33807
(Many engine and interior shots in color; publishes other excellent car magazines)

Special Interest Autos
P.O. Box 196
Bennington, VT 05201-9990
(Wide range of cars)

Index

Edited by Joann E. Woy